LUCCA
TRAVEL GUIDE 2024-2025

Exploring Tuscany Historic Walls and Family-Friendly Sites

TARA D. SMITH

Copyright © 2024 by TARA D. SMITH

All rights reserved. No part of this book may be reproduced in any form or by any electronic or mechanical means, including information storage and retrieval systems, without permission in writing from the publisher, except by a reviewer who may quote brief passages in a review.

MAP OF LUCCA

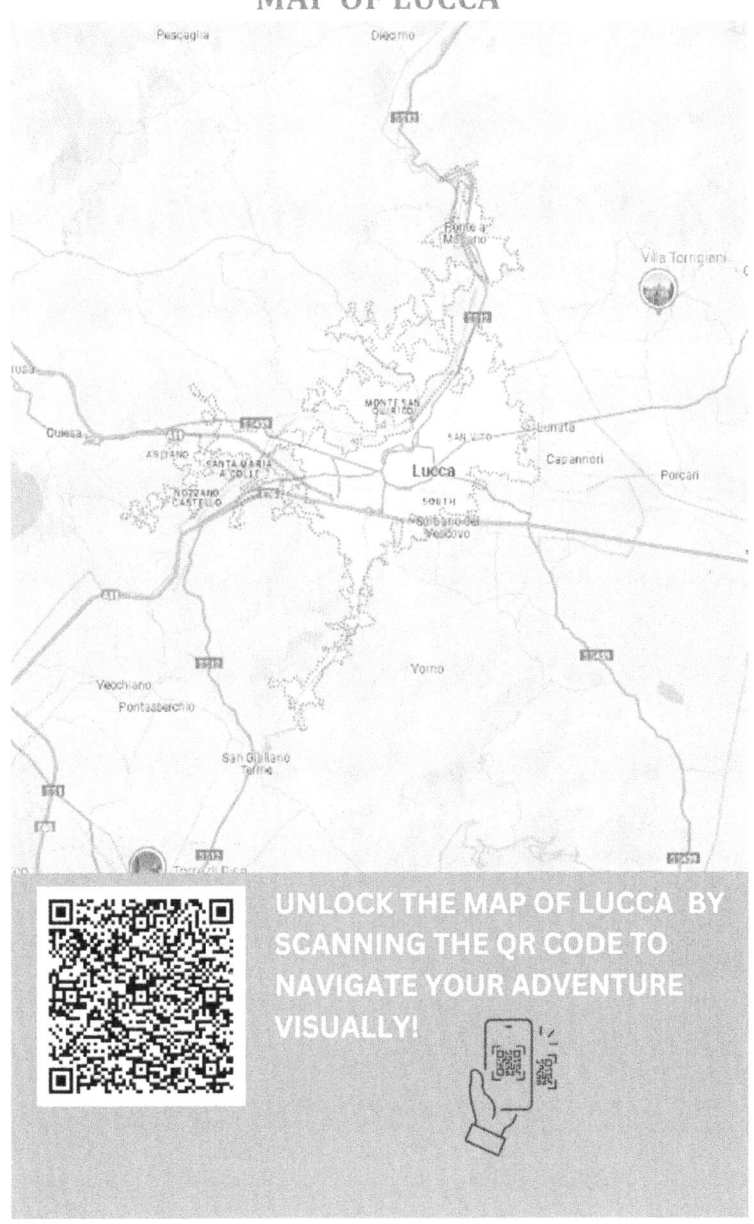

UNLOCK THE MAP OF LUCCA BY SCANNING THE QR CODE TO NAVIGATE YOUR ADVENTURE VISUALLY!

TABLE OF CONTENTS

INTRODUCTION 9

   Overview of Lucca 10

   History and Culture 12

GETTING TO LUCCA 16

   Transportation Options 17

   Airports and Train Stations 20

   Driving and parking 27

ACCOMMODATION IN LUCCA 30

   Hotels and Resorts 31

   Bed and Breakfasts 44

   Rental Apartments 53

EXPLORING LUCCA 62

   Top Attractions 63

   Historic Sites 82

   Museums and Galleries 98

   Parks and Gardens 101

DINING AND NIGHTLIFE 106

Traditional Tuscan Cuisine 107

Local Restaurants and Cafés 118

Wine Bars and Pubs 123

Evening Entertainment 126

SHOPPING IN LUCCA 130

Markets and Bazaars 131

Artisanal Crafts and Souvenirs 132

Fashion Boutiques and Designer Stores 137

OUTDOOR ACTIVITIES 140

Cycling and Walking Tours 141

Hiking and Nature Trails 146

River Activities and Boat Tours 151

KID-FRIENDLY ATTRACTIONS IN LUCCA 154

Family-Friendly Accommodation Options 155

Tips for Traveling with Children 162

Educational and Interactive Activities for Kids 167

DAY TRIPS FROM LUCCA 173

Pisa 174

5

Florence 176

Cinque Terre 178

PRACTICAL INFORMATION 183

Weather and Climate 184

Currency and Payment 187

Language and Communication 190

Safety Tips and Emergency Contacts 193

LUCCA
TRAVEL GUIDE 2024

TARA D. SMITH

WELCOME TO LUCCA

- Overview of Lucca
- History and Culture

INTRODUCTION

Ah, let me tell you about Lucca! It's a gem, a sparkling jewel nestled right here in Tuscany! Imagine, cobbled streets that whisper secrets of centuries past, a grand city wall that you can walk right on top of, and piazzas that come alive with the sound of laughter and clinking glasses every single evening. Forget the noisy cars, here you can wander freely, taking in the scent of fresh bread baking from hidden alleys and the sweet perfume of jasmine climbing up ancient stone walls.

But Lucca's not just about charming streets and delicious smells! Oh no, this city has a heart that beats with history! Towers that reach for the sky, churches adorned with golden mosaics, and even a Roman amphitheater hiding in plain sight – there's a story around every corner. And the people, my friends, the people of Lucca! Warm smiles, a love for good food and conversation, they'll welcome you with open arms and make you feel right at home.

Whether you're a history buff, a foodie at heart, or simply someone who craves a taste of la dolce vita, Lucca has something for you. So, pack your bags, lace up your walking shoes, and get ready for an adventure you won't soon forget! Lucca awaits, and trust me, it will leave you breathless!

Overview of Lucca

Ancient Origins: Lucca's beginnings can be traced back to the Etruscans, an ancient civilization preceding the Romans. Later, it prospered under Roman governance, with remnants such as an amphitheater still standing in the Piazza dell'Anfiteatro.

Medieval Power: During the Middle Ages, Lucca emerged as a significant city-state. For close to five centuries, it flourished as an independent republic, repelling assaults with its impressive defensive walls, which remain remarkably intact today.

Changing Fortunes: Lucca's fate shifted over the centuries. During the Napoleonic era, it briefly came under the rule of Napoleon's sister, Elisa Bonaparte Baciocchi. Eventually, in 1847, it became part of the Grand Duchy of Tuscany and later, a unified Italy.

A Delight for the Senses: Unveiling Lucca's Charm

Architectural Wonders: Lucca showcases a captivating variety of architectural styles. Explore the Romanesque splendor of the Lucca Cathedral, or marvel at the Guinigi Tower, a distinctive leaning tower crowned with holm oak trees.

Artistic Pleasures: Immerse yourself in Lucca's rich artistic heritage. Visit the birth home of the renowned composer Giacomo Puccini, now transformed into a museum dedicated to his life and works. Art aficionados can explore the collections at the National Museum of Palazzo Mansi.

A Dynamic City: Unlike many other hilltop Tuscan towns, Lucca benefits from a flat terrain, making it ideal for exploration on foot or by bicycle. The wide, tree-lined pathways atop the city walls offer a picturesque route for a leisurely stroll or an invigorating bike ride.

Beyond the Boundaries: Discovering Lucca's Surroundings

Musical Interludes: Lucca has become a haven for music enthusiasts. The Lucca Summer Festival draws acclaimed international artists, while October sees the city come alive with Lucca Comics & Games, a prominent European event celebrating comics, animation, and role-playing games.

Culinary Delights: Treat your palate to the culinary delights of Lucca. Sample local specialties like "farro," an ancient grain incorporated into various dishes, or indulge in "torta di cecco," a delectable rice cake. And of course, accompany your meal with a glass of the region's renowned wines.

Gateway to Exploration: Lucca serves as a gateway to further adventures. Explore the beauty of the Versilian coast with its sandy beaches, or venture into the Apuan Alps, a paradise for hikers and nature enthusiasts.

History and Culture

This quaint town is a captivating journey through time, adorned with medieval architecture and steeped in history at every turn – from the cobblestones to the statues, arches, and towers. It conjures tales of castles, knights, and enchanted realms, where fortresses and royal gardens flourish.

Lucca's story traces back over two millennia, to its foundation by the Romans in 180 BC. They established the initial settlement, and in 1118, Lucca gained status as a Comune, leading to the construction of a second set of walls that incorporated the original Roman fortifications. By the 1300s, the city had expanded and fortified further with a third set of walls to repel potential invaders.

Typically, fortified cities boasted four main gates, each aligned with a cardinal direction. However, Lucca defied convention with only three gates – north, west, and south – omitting an eastern entrance as a symbolic declaration of independence from Florence, its perennial adversary. This stance was a subtle nod to the city's autonomy from Firenze and the influential Medici Family.

Renowned for its silk production, Lucca thrived as a trade hub from the late 12th century onward, exporting its luxurious fabric to the Western world. This lucrative commerce elevated Lucca's status, fostering strong alliances with the Pope and prominent European families, allowing the city to remain unscathed by conflict.

For over 700 years, Lucca stood as an independent entity, resilient against conquest until Napoleon's brief occupation during the French First Empire. Under his rule, the fourth, eastern gate, dubbed "Porta Elisa" in honor of Napoleon's sister and Grand Duchess of Tuscany, Elisa, was erected.

The monumental walls that encircle Lucca today trace their origins to the Renaissance period, dating back to the 17th century. Notably, these walls are unique in Italy for being entirely accessible on foot, by bicycle, or by car, albeit limited to police vehicles traversing the elevated pathways

Lucca boasts with pride its status as the birthplace of the renowned opera composer Giacomo Puccini. In a family steeped in musical heritage, Puccini himself gifted the world with timeless masterpieces such as La Bohème, Tosca, and Madame Butterfly. The city honors this legacy through the esteemed Puccini Festival, a gathering revered by opera enthusiasts worldwide.

For history enthusiasts and art connoisseurs alike, Lucca offers a wealth of museums and galleries to explore. The

Museo Nazionale di Palazzo Mansi captivates with its collection of Renaissance paintings, while the Villa Guinigi National Museum unveils a trove of archaeological treasures. The picturesque Piazza dell'Anfiteatro, nestled within the elliptical remains of a Roman amphitheater, beckons visitors with its charm.

The city's rich religious heritage is embodied in its magnificent cathedral, the Duomo, which shelters the revered Volto Santo, a cedar-wood crucifix believed to date back to the time of Christ. Each September, Lucca radiates with the brilliance of the Luminara di Santa Croce, a mesmerizing spectacle where countless candles illuminate buildings and streets.

Beyond its historical and religious landmarks, Lucca's cultural allure extends to its intact city walls, providing a unique promenade around the town. Moreover, Lucca delights food enthusiasts with its array of local delicacies, including the celebrated artisanal gelato.

GETTING TO LUCCA

- Transportation Options
- Airports and Train Stations
- Driving and parking

GETTING TO LUCCA

Transportation Options

Getting to Lucca is convenient whether you're traveling by car or public transportation, thanks to its strategic location along major highways and railway lines linking Florence, Pisa, and Viareggio.

By Car:

The historic center of Lucca prohibits vehicular access, with many areas reserved exclusively for residents. Visitors must park outside the walls, though a few designated parking areas exist within. Look for signage indicating parking availability for non-residents. Lucca sits on the A11 Firenze-Mare highway, connecting Florence to Pisa and the Versilia Coast. Take either the Lucca Est or Ovest exits if arriving from the north or south. If coming from the coast on the A12 Genova-Roma highway, connect at Viareggio before heading to Lucca Ovest via the Bretella road (tolls apply). Both Lucca highway exits are approximately 1 km from the city center.

By Train:

Trains offer a straightforward and efficient means of reaching Lucca. Maintaining a consistent routine makes travel planning simple. Upon arrival, explore the city on foot or by bike (details on bike rentals below). The Lucca train station, situated in Piazza Ricasoli, is a brief five-minute walk from Porta San Pietro, one of the entry points to the city's historic center. Lucca is well-connected via train lines linking Florence to Viareggio and Florence (or Pistoia) to Pisa, with numerous daily departures to and from Lucca. Pisa is a short 15–20-minute ride away, while Florence takes approximately an hour and 20 minutes and Viareggio about 20 minutes. Other popular Tuscan destinations along the same train line include Pistoia (approximately 45 minutes away) and Montecatini Terme (less than half an hour). Daily trains from Lucca also serve Garfagnana.

From Pisa airport, take a train to Pisa Centrale station, then transfer to a train bound for Lucca (or look for a train to Florence/Viareggio that stops in Lucca). From Florence airport, travel to the Florence city center train station (Santa Maria Novella) by bus (departing every 30 minutes) or taxi (approximately 25€), then catch a train or bus to Lucca.

By Bus:

The bus station, operated by VaiBus, is located within the city walls at Piazzale Verdi. Florence, Pisa, and Viareggio are among the Tuscan cities connected to Lucca by bus. However, bus rides typically take longer than trains, so travelers may find trains a more convenient option.

To reach Lucca, travelers have several options, including bus, train, and car. Lucca's historic center, known as the "centro storico," is largely pedestrianized, making walking the easiest mode of transportation from parking areas, the train station, or bus stops.

By Bus, Train, or Car:

When in Tuscany, a visit to Lucca is a highlight. The city, surrounded by intact fortified walls, boasts a rich history dating back to its founding by the Etruscans and later becoming a Roman Colony in 180 BC. The remnants of the Roman city are evident in Lucca's layout, with highlights such as the oval "Piazza dell'Anfiteatro" inspired by the ancient Roman amphitheater. Throughout its history, Lucca has been a powerful independent commune and a favorite of Napoleon, who bestowed the city upon his sister.

Airports and Train Stations

Which Airport to Fly to for Lucca?

While there is no airport in Lucca, Pisa Airport is the closest and most convenient option. Other nearby airports include Florence, Bologna, Rome, and Genoa. Here are the travel times to Lucca from the closest airports:

Getting to Lucca by Train:

Train travel is an excellent option due to Lucca's pedestrianized center. You can explore the city on foot or by renting a bike or taking a taxi.

Where to buy train tickets in Italy:

There are several websites, but Trainline.com is a reliable option that works across Europe. Remember to stamp your ticket before boarding using the special machines called "obliterators."

How to Get to Lucca from Pisa by Train:

From Pisa Airport, take the PisaMover to the central station, then a direct train to Lucca (about 22 to 27 minutes, €4).

How to Take a Train from Florence to Lucca:

From Florence Airport, take the T2 Vespucci tram to Florence's main station, then a train to Lucca (about 1 hr 40 min, starting at €9).

How to Travel by Train from Bologna or Rome to Lucca:

From Rome or Bologna, take a train to Florence, then follow the instructions above.

How to Take the Train from Genoa Airport to Lucca:

Take the VolaBus shuttle to Genoa Station, then a train to Lucca (about 2 hr 20 min, €17.00).

Getting to Lucca by Train from Perugia Airport:

From Perugia Airport, take a bus to Perugia Train Station, then a train to Lucca (about 4 hr, €26).

How to Get from the Train Station into the Center of Lucca:

Lucca's train station is close to the center, with easy walking access. Alternatively, buses are available for those who prefer.

To travel from Pisa to Lucca by train, follow these steps:

- ❖ The train offers a convenient option to travel from Pisa to Lucca.
- ❖ Upon arrival at the airport, take the PisaMover to the main central station. Exit arrivals and head left to find the PisaMover, located at the end of the airport.
- ❖ The journey from the airport to the central station takes approximately 5 minutes.
- ❖ From the central station, you can board a direct train to Lucca. The trip typically lasts between 22 to 27 minutes and costs around €4 (four EUR).

Note that you cannot purchase tickets for the PisaMover at the main railway station. Separate ticket machines are available at the PisaMover itself.

How to get to Lucca by train from Florence:

- If you arrive at Florence Airport, you can take the T2 Vespucci tram into the center of Florence.
- Purchase a ticket for the tram at the stop from an automatic machine. Contactless cards are accepted, and a one-way ticket costs €1.70.
- The tram journey from the airport to the main Florence railway station, Santa Maria Novella, takes approximately 20 minutes.
- From Florence Santa Maria Novella, board a train to Lucca station. The journey usually involves a change in Pistoia and takes around 1 hour and 40 minutes. Ticket prices start at around €9 one way.

Rail travel to Lucca from Bologna or Rome:

- To reach Lucca from Rome or Bologna, first travel to Florence using very fast trains that run from both cities.
- A fast train from Rome to Florence takes about 1 hour and 40 minutes and costs from €20 (or €28.90 for First Class Travel).

- A fast train from Bologna to Florence takes around 40 minutes and costs from €18.90. A slower train takes about 1 hour and 45 minutes and costs under €10.
- From Florence, follow the instructions above to reach Lucca by train.

Getting to Lucca by train from Genoa Airport:

- At Genoa Airport, take the shuttle called "VolaBus" to Genoa Station, Genova Piazza Principe. The shuttle ride lasts 30 minutes and operates every 40 minutes. Alternatively, you may choose to take a taxi.
- From Genoa Station, board a train to Lucca. The journey takes around 2 hours and 20 minutes, with a change in Viareggio, and costs approximately €17.00.

How to get to Lucca from Perugia Airport:

- From Perugia Airport, take a bus to Perugia Train Station.
- From Perugia Train Station, board a train to Lucca. The journey takes just over 4 hours, with a couple of changes, and costs around €26.

How to get into Lucca Centre from the Train Station:

Lucca's train station is conveniently close to the city center, allowing for an easy walk to reach popular landmarks such as Piazza Napoleone, San Michele in Foro, and Piazza dell'anfiteatro. Alternatively, buses run into the city center for those who prefer public transportation, especially when traveling with young children.

To travel to Lucca by car, keep in mind the following tips:

Restricted Access

Lucca's historic city center is closed off to traffic, and many areas allowing cars are exclusively reserved for residents. Be cautious of red-circle no-entry signs, indicating areas restricted to residents only. These zones, known as ZTL (Zona Traffico Limitato), are often monitored by video cameras that issue fines to unauthorized vehicles. Avoid entering these restricted zones to prevent fines.

Directions

Directions to Lucca via road signs are well-marked, especially on main roads. Lucca is conveniently located near the A11 Motorway, also known as the Firenze - Mare, a fast road connecting Florence with Pisa and the Versilia Coast. If traveling from the North or South, take the A11 and exit at Lucca Est or Ovest.

From Airports

If arriving at Pisa or Florence airports and renting a car, follow signs to the A11 Motorway in both cases to reach Lucca.

Parking

Once in Lucca, park your vehicle outside the city walls, as the historic center is pedestrianized. While there are a few parking areas inside the walls, be sure to read signs indicating whether parking is open to everyone.

Here are some recommended parking lots in Lucca:

- ❖ Parcheggio Mazzini: Located on Via dei Bacchettoni, near Piazza dell'Anfiteatro.

- ❖ Parcheggio Stazione: Situated at Piazzale B. Ricasoli, near the railway station.
- ❖ Parcheggio Cittadella: Found on Via della Cittadella, suitable for accessing the city center (note narrow access).
- ❖ Parcheggio Via del Peso: Located on Via del Peso, near Piazza Napoleone.

Generally, upon entering these parking lots, take a ticket, and pay at a machine upon your return. Parking charges are typically reasonable, around €2 per hour or €35 for a day.

Driving and parking

Parking in Lucca requires careful attention to regulations to avoid fines or towing. Here are some essential tips:

Paid Parking

No outside parking is available for non-residents... Assume that parking inside the walls requires payment at parking meters, usually located within 100 meters of where you've parked.

Paid parking spaces are indicated by blue lines. Avoid parking in spaces marked with yellow lines, as these are reserved for residents.

Traffic Zones

Lucca is divided into traffic zones A and B. Unless you're dropping off or picking up bags at your hotel, avoid entering either zone with your car. Look for signs with a red circle and the words "zona pedonale" to indicate pedestrian-only streets.

Be cautious of areas labeled as "ZTL" (limited traffic zone), marked with white letters on the road. These zones are monitored by video cameras, and entering without permission will result in fines. Only residents with parking permits are allowed to enter these areas.

Recommended Parking Lots

Inside the walls, parking lots with large capacities include Mazzini, Lorenzini, Cittadella, and Piazza Santa Maria.

Note that the parking lot in Piazza San Francesco has recently been reduced to side street parking, decreasing the chances of finding a spot.

Parking Outside the Historical Center

If parking outside the historical center by the walls, ensure you park in marked spaces and avoid parking on the grass to avoid receiving a ticket.

Dealing with Parking Tickets

If you receive a parking ticket, you can pay it at the post office located on the intersection of via Valisisneri and via delle Trombe. Ensure you have proof of payment.

In rare cases of towing, contact the municipal police at tel. 0583 44 2727. You must pay the fine in full and provide proof of payment to retrieve your car.

By following these guidelines, you can navigate parking in Lucca smoothly and avoid any unwanted fines or inconveniences.

ACCOMMODATION IN LUCCA

- Hotels and Resorts
- Bed and Breakfasts
- Rental Apartments

ACCOMMODATION IN LUCCA

Hotels and Resorts

Hotel Ilaria

Daily Price: The daily rates at Hotel Ilaria span from €84 to €650, accommodating travelers with varying budgetary considerations.

Hotel Ilaria, nestled within the heart of Lucca, invites guests to experience its tranquil and refined ambiance amid the city's historic backdrop. Here's a glimpse into the offerings of this delightful 4-star establishment:

Rooms: Featuring 41 rooms, Hotel Ilaria provides a range of accommodations to suit diverse preferences and budgets. From standard rooms to luxurious suites, guests can anticipate comfort and elegance throughout their stay.

Location: Positioned in Lucca's city center, Hotel Ilaria grants convenient access to the town's famed Renaissance streets and attractions. Guests can effortlessly explore the historic city and immerse themselves in its rich cultural heritage.

Amenities:

Free WiFi: Stay connected throughout your visit with complimentary WiFi access.

Complimentary Breakfast Buffets: Begin your day with a delightful breakfast spread, included with your stay.

Bicycle Rental: Explore Lucca's picturesque streets with the hotel's complimentary bicycle rental service.

Terrace and Hot Tub: Unwind on the terrace while indulging in complimentary snacks and drinks. Take a relaxing soak in the hot tub and admire the view of the lush gardens, offering a serene retreat after a day of exploration.

Tranquil Atmosphere: Occupying the historic stables of Villa Buonvisi and a 14th-century church, Hotel Ilaria emanates a peaceful ambiance, providing guests with a serene environment to rejuvenate.

Modern Comforts: The spacious and tastefully furnished rooms are equipped with modern amenities, ensuring a comfortable and enjoyable stay for guests.

Convenient Location: Hotel Ilaria enjoys proximity to the city's main attractions and transportation options, facilitating easy exploration of Lucca's highlights.

During your trip, you'll find a range of amenities and services available at the hotel:

Parking is provided on-site for a fee of €20 per day. Valet parking and electric vehicle charging stations are also available, along with accessible parking options.

Enjoy complimentary Wi-Fi throughout the hotel, ensuring you stay connected during your stay.

Rooms are equipped with air conditioning, private bathrooms featuring amenities such as toiletries, a hairdryer, and either a bath or shower. Some rooms also offer bidets for added convenience.

Though fees may apply, pets are welcome at the accommodation.

Indulge in various activities offered by the hotel, including bicycle rental, live sports events broadcast, cooking classes, happy hours, bike tours, walking tours, movie nights, and temporary art galleries. Additionally, explore nearby attractions with options for cycling and hiking.

Relax in the sun terrace or outdoor furniture areas, and take advantage of the hotel's pet-friendly policy.

Satisfy your culinary cravings with food and drink options such as a coffee house on-site, fruits, wine/champagne (additional charge), special diet menus upon request, a snack bar, breakfast in the room, a bar, and a minibar.

For entertainment, enjoy a flat-screen TV with satellite channels, telephone access, and various activities organized by the hotel.

Benefit from reception services including private check-in/check-out, concierge assistance, luggage storage, tour desk access, and 24-hour front desk availability.

Ensure a comfortable stay with daily housekeeping, ironing service, dry cleaning, and laundry facilities available upon request.

Business travelers can utilize fax/photocopying services and meeting/banquet facilities (additional charge).

For safety and security, the hotel features fire extinguishers, CCTV surveillance, smoke alarms, key card access, 24-hour security, and safety deposit boxes.

General amenities include shuttle service (additional charge), pet bowls, grocery deliveries (additional charge), a shared lounge/TV area, vending machines for snacks and drinks, designated smoking areas, allergy-free rooms, heating, car hire options, packed lunches, soundproof rooms, a lift, family rooms, facilities for disabled guests, airport shuttle service (additional charge), non-smoking rooms, and room service.

Relax and rejuvenate with wellness facilities such as sun umbrellas, sun loungers or beach chairs, a hot tub/jacuzzi, and a solarium.

Communicate comfortably with multilingual staff fluent in German, English, Spanish, French, and Italian.

Hotel Palazzo Alexander

Via Santa Giustina 48, Lucca

Prices start at £123 per night

At Palazzo Alexander, accommodation features antique wood floors and marble bathrooms, adding a touch of elegance to your stay. Complimentary internet access is provided in communal areas, ensuring you stay connected throughout your visit.

Start your day with an American buffet breakfast, showcasing fresh and locally sourced produce. Indulge in a variety of options to fuel up for your adventures in Lucca.

Relax and unwind at the hotel's bar, where you can enjoy a refreshing drink in a cozy atmosphere.

Conveniently situated just inside Lucca's historic walls, Palazzo Alexander offers easy access to iconic landmarks such as Lucca Cathedral and Guinigi Tower, both within a leisurely 10-minute walk. Explore the rich history and charm of the city right from your doorstep.

The property offers a range of facilities tailored to enhance your trip experience. Enjoy the convenience of private parking available nearby upon reservation, ensuring your vehicle is secure during your stay.

Accommodations are equipped with air conditioning, ensuring a comfortable environment regardless of the weather. Each room features a private bathroom stocked with essential amenities, including free toiletries, towels, and a hairdryer. Some rooms also boast additional comforts such as a minibar and tea/coffee maker.

For families or larger groups, family rooms are available, providing ample space for everyone to relax and unwind.

Indulge in various activities offered by the property, including bicycle rental to explore the surrounding area or participate in local cultural tours. For those seeking relaxation, enjoy a full-body massage or unwind with a selection of books, DVDs, or music available for children.

Start your day with a delicious breakfast served in the comfort of your room or at the onsite bar, offering a range of beverages and snacks throughout the day.

Convenient services such as private check-in/check-out, luggage storage, and concierge assistance are provided to ensure a seamless stay. For business travelers, fax/photocopying services are available upon request.

Rest assured with safety measures in place, including fire extinguishers, security alarms, and 24-hour security surveillance. The property is also equipped with accessibility features such as elevators for easy access to upper floors.

With its array of amenities and services, the property aims to provide a memorable and comfortable stay for guests from around the world. Languages spoken by the staff include German, English, Spanish, French, and Italian, ensuring clear communication and assistance throughout your visit.

Hotel San Marco

Via San Marco 368, 55100, Lucca Italy

Prices start at $142 per night

Hotel San Marco offers a welcoming atmosphere and a range of amenities to ensure a pleasant stay for travelers visiting Lucca. The rooms are equipped with modern comforts including a flat-screen TV, air conditioning, and a minibar, providing exceptional comfort and convenience. Guests can also stay connected with free Wi-Fi available throughout the hotel.

Convenience is key at Hotel San Marco, with amenities such as concierge service and room service available to cater to guests' needs. Additionally, guests can enjoy a refreshing swim in the pool and start their day with a complimentary breakfast, adding to the overall special experience of their stay.

For guests arriving by car, free parking is available onsite, offering added convenience and peace of mind. The hotel's convenient location makes it easy to explore popular landmarks such as Via Fillungo and Basilica of San Frediano, both located just a short distance away.

During their stay, guests can also explore nearby restaurants, offering a variety of dining options within walking distance of the hotel. Whether indulging in fine dining at L'Imbuto or enjoying traditional Italian cuisine at Buca di Sant'Antonio, there is something to suit every palate.

Overall, Hotel San Marco provides a comfortable and convenient base for travelers to enjoy all that Lucca has to offer, whether it's sightseeing, dining, or simply relaxing in the welcoming ambiance of the hotel.

Hotel amenities at Hotel San Marco cater to the comfort and convenience of guests, offering a range of features to enhance their stay. Guests can take advantage of free parking and complimentary high-speed internet access throughout the property, ensuring connectivity during their visit. For relaxation and leisure, the hotel boasts a refreshing outdoor pool where guests can unwind and enjoy the sun.

Start the day right with a complimentary breakfast buffet served to all guests, providing a delicious array of options to fuel up for the day ahead. Those looking to explore the area can opt for bicycle rental services offered by the hotel, perfect for discovering the local attractions and scenic surroundings.

Pets are welcome at Hotel San Marco, making it a pet-friendly accommodation option for travelers accompanied by their furry friends. Business travelers can make use of the on-site business center, equipped with internet access, while baggage storage facilities are available for added convenience.

The hotel's bar and lounge area provide a relaxed setting to enjoy a refreshing drink, while the poolside bar offers a picturesque spot to unwind with a beverage. Additional services such as concierge assistance, dry cleaning, and laundry service are also available to meet guests' needs.

Room features include air conditioning for comfort, along with amenities such as room service, a safe, telephone, minibar, refrigerator, flatscreen TV, and a hairdryer. The hotel offers a variety of room types including non-smoking rooms, suites, and family rooms to accommodate different preferences and group sizes.

Hotel San Marco is classified as a mid-range establishment and is situated in a residential neighborhood, offering guests a quiet and relaxed environment during their stay. The hotel staff is multilingual, speaking English, French, German, and Italian, ensuring effective communication and assistance for international guests.

Alla Corte Degli Angeli

Via Degli Angeli 23 Centro Storico, 55100, Lucca Italy

21 rooms from £133 per night

This charming and inviting hotel, located within Lucca's old walls, is only a ten-minute walk from the cathedral. The Hotel Alla Corte degli Angeli's attractions include attractively appointed rooms and free Wi-Fi.

Some include wood-beamed ceilings and frescoes on the walls.

Among the many modern amenities in your room are an LCD TV with Sky channels and an iPod docking station.

Alla Corte degli Angeli has a bar and a 24-hour reception.

Offering a range of convenient amenities, this property ensures a comfortable stay in Lucca. Guests can enjoy free WiFi and air conditioning throughout their accommodation, along with private bathrooms equipped with toiletries, towels, and hairdryers. The rooms feature flat-screen TVs with satellite channels, as well as desks for work or leisure.

Outdoor spaces include a garden, perfect for relaxation. Pets are welcome upon request at no extra charge, and private parking is available on-site for a fee.

The property also offers various services such as concierge assistance, luggage storage, and express check-in/check-out. For business travelers, fax/photocopying facilities are available. Safety measures include fire extinguishers, smoke alarms, and 24-hour security.

Guests can enjoy breakfast in the room or at the bar, where wine and champagne are also available for an additional charge. Additional services include daily housekeeping, laundry, dry cleaning, and ironing services, all provided for an extra fee. Shuttle service and airport shuttle can be arranged upon request.

The property features allergy-free rooms, soundproofing, and a lift for accessibility. It caters to families with amenities like pet baskets and shared lounge areas. Languages spoken by the staff include English, Spanish, French, Italian, and Romanian.

Bed and Breakfasts

Bed and breakfast accommodations offer a unique and intimate experience for travelers seeking a cozy retreat. Hosts open their homes to guests, providing comfortable private rooms and a complimentary breakfast to start the day. While the accommodations typically offer a more personalized touch, it's common for bathrooms to be shared among guests, fostering a sense of community. Additionally, guests often have the opportunity to interact with the hosts and enjoy shared spaces, creating a warm and welcoming atmosphere conducive to relaxation and connection.

1. B&B Anfiteatro

Via Dell'Anfiteatro 25, Lucca

B&B Anfiteatro enjoys a prime location overlooking the ancient ruins of the Roman amphitheatre right in the heart of Lucca. Its elegant rooms boast charming exposed wood-beamed ceilings and offer the convenience of free WiFi. Just steps away, guests can explore the bustling Via Fillungo shopping street, adding to the allure of this central location.

Each of the air-conditioned rooms at B&B Anfiteatro is tastefully appointed and features a satellite TV for entertainment. The private bathrooms are equipped with showers and hairdryers, ensuring guests' comfort during their stay.

In the mornings, guests are treated to a delicious breakfast served at a nearby partner restaurant, providing a delightful start to the day. For those in need of a caffeine boost or a relaxing cup of tea, coffee and tea are readily available in the property's shared lounge area.

Conveniently situated just 160 metres from the Basilica of San Frediano and a short 5-minute walk from the Church of San Francesco, B&B Anfiteatro offers easy access to some of Lucca's most iconic landmarks, allowing guests to immerse themselves in the rich history and culture of this charming city.

B&B Anfiteatro offers a range of facilities tailored to enhance your stay. The property features a restaurant where guests can enjoy delicious meals, complemented by complimentary Wi-Fi access throughout. Air conditioning ensures a comfortable environment in each room, all of which boast private bathrooms for added convenience. Families are catered to with spacious family rooms available.

The bathrooms are well-equipped with essential amenities such as toiletries, towels, and hairdryers. Guests can enjoy refreshing showers in the modern bath or shower facilities provided. The bedrooms are furnished with comfortable linen and ample storage space in wardrobes or closets. Views of the inner courtyard or the charming city enhance the ambiance of the rooms.

For those who prefer to prepare their own meals, a shared kitchen is available, complete with cleaning products and a toaster. Additionally, room amenities include practical features like sockets near the bed and fold-up beds for added flexibility.

Guests can relax or catch up on work in the living area, which includes a desk and a flat-screen TV for entertainment. Other media and technology options include radios and TVs in the rooms.

Food and drink options at the B&B include the availability of wine or champagne, as well as special diet menus upon request. The property also offers services such as shared lounge areas, private check-in and check-out, luggage storage, and fax/photocopying facilities. Packed lunches are available for guests on the go, and express check-in/check-out services streamline the arrival and departure process.

Safety and security measures include the provision of fire extinguishers and key access. The property is entirely non-smoking and features air conditioning, heating, and soundproof rooms for added comfort. Languages spoken by the staff include English, Spanish, and Italian, ensuring effective communication and assistance for guests from various backgrounds.

2- Corte Meraviglia - Relais

Via Antonio Mordini 63, Lucca

Nestled in the heart of Lucca, Corte Meraviglia - Relais offers a charming bed and breakfast experience with a range of convenient amenities. Guests can take advantage of private parking and complimentary WiFi during their stay, while also enjoying the tranquil ambiance of the garden and the convenience of an on-site bar.

The property's prime location provides easy access to notable landmarks such as the Guinigi Tower and Piazza dell'Anfiteatro. Guests can also enjoy picturesque garden and inner courtyard views from the comfort of their accommodations. Additionally, the famous Leaning Tower of Pisa is just 20 km away.

Corte Meraviglia - Relais offers a variety of room options, including family rooms and units with private entrances. Some accommodations feature additional amenities such as terraces, dressing rooms, and seating areas with TVs. Air conditioning and heating ensure a comfortable stay year-round, while certain units also offer coffee machines and options for wine or champagne.

Guests can start their day with a visit to the on-site coffee shop or opt for packed lunches for added convenience. A shared lounge area provides a relaxing space for guests to unwind and socialize during their stay.

For those looking to explore further afield, Piazza dei Miracoli is just 22 km away, and San Michele in Foro is a mere 500 meters from the property. Transportation to and from the airport is made easy with the option of a paid airport shuttle service, with Pisa International Airport located 37 km away.

Conveniently located in the heart of Lucca, this property offers a range of amenities suitable for various types of travelers. Guests can benefit from on-site parking and complimentary WiFi throughout their stay. Each accommodation features a private bathroom and flat-screen TV, ensuring comfort and convenience for guests. Families can opt for family rooms, while outdoor enthusiasts can enjoy the picnic area, sun terrace, and garden.

For those seeking entertainment, the property offers activities such as happy hour, walking tours, movie nights, and pub crawls. Additionally, guests can explore nearby temporary art galleries for a cultural experience.

The property boasts a coffee house and bar, providing guests with options for refreshments. High-speed WiFi ensures seamless connectivity, with speeds suitable for streaming and video calls on multiple devices.

Parking is available nearby for a daily fee, and accessible parking options are provided. Reception services include private check-in/check-out, luggage storage, and express check-in/check-out for added convenience.

Families traveling with young children can request strollers, while cleaning services such as daily housekeeping, ironing, and laundry are available.

Safety and security measures include fire extinguishers, security alarms, and key access. Guests can also enjoy shared lounge areas and access to packed lunches. Airport shuttle services are available for an additional charge, and the property offers non-smoking rooms and multilingual staff fluent in English, Spanish, French, and Italian.

3- IN LUCUS Guest House

33 Via Elisa, Lucca

IN LUCUS Guest House, situated in Lucca, offers comfortable accommodation with air conditioning and private bathrooms. The property enjoys city views and is conveniently located within walking distance of several attractions, including Guinigi Tower and Piazza dell'Anfiteatro. San Michele in Foro is also nearby, providing guests with easy access to the city center and its bustling atmosphere. Additionally, the Leaning Tower of Pisa is just 20 km away.

Each unit at the guest house features essential amenities such as a wardrobe, flat-screen TV, and free WiFi. The private bathrooms come with a bidet and hairdryer for added convenience. Guests can also make use of the provided fridge during their stay.

For guests' convenience, a minimarket is available onsite, offering essential supplies. Nearby attractions include Piazza Napoleone, less than 1 km away, and Marlia Villa Reale, situated 8.8 km from the property. Pisa International Airport is the nearest airport, located 37 km from IN LUCUS Guest House.

The property offers essential amenities for a comfortable stay, including free Wi-Fi and air conditioning in each room, ensuring guests stay connected and cool throughout their visit. Private bathrooms are provided, equipped with toiletries, a hairdryer, and a shower for convenience. Guests can enjoy city views from their rooms, which also feature flat-screen TVs for entertainment.

Rooms are well-appointed with wardrobes or closets, and some offer additional amenities like refrigerators for added convenience. Daily housekeeping ensures that the accommodation remains clean and tidy throughout guests' stay.

For guests' peace of mind, safety measures such as fire extinguishers and key access are in place. The property also features a minimarket onsite, providing added convenience for guests' needs. The staff are fluent in

English and Italian, providing assistance and guidance throughout guests' stay.

Rental Apartments

For those who value independence and privacy during their travels, an apartment or flat serves as an ideal retreat. These accommodations offer fully furnished rooms and kitchen facilities, providing guests with the flexibility to unwind individually or gather together for meals and planning sessions. Whether traveling with family or friends, apartments provide ample space for relaxation and the opportunity to create memorable moments together. Available for both short-term stays and extended visits, these accommodations offer a home away from home experience, allowing guests to immerse themselves fully in their destination's culture and lifestyle.

1- Casa i Galli

Via Case Galli 55, 05013 Castel Giorgio Italy

Price $ (Based on Average Nightly Rates for a Standard Room from our Partners)

Located conveniently in the heart of Lucca, Casa i Galli offers guests the perfect blend of comfort and convenience. Within close proximity to notable attractions like San Michele in Foro and Piazza Napoleone, this property provides free WiFi and essential amenities such as air conditioning, a dishwasher, and a coffee machine. The apartment boasts quiet street views and features a soundproof design, ensuring a peaceful stay.

The spacious apartment comprises two bedrooms, a well-appointed bathroom, bed linen, towels, and a range of modern conveniences including a flat-screen TV with streaming services. Guests can enjoy meals in the dining area or on the terrace, which offers captivating city views. Additionally, a balcony serves as an outdoor dining area, providing a charming space to savor al fresco dining experiences.

For added comfort, the apartment is allergy-free and designated as non-smoking. Guests can start their day with a delicious buffet or Italian breakfast featuring fresh pastries and juice, served daily at the apartment. With its central location and comfortable amenities, Casa i Galli offers a delightful retreat for travelers exploring Lucca and its surroundings.

For your convenience, this property offers a range of amenities suitable for your trip. Parking is available nearby, and for those who prefer to relax outdoors, there's a balcony to enjoy the city views. Stay connected with free Wi-Fi throughout the accommodation, and keep cool with air conditioning in every room. Enjoy the privacy of your own bathroom, complete with toiletries, towels, and a hairdryer.

The kitchen is fully equipped with essential appliances including a coffee machine, oven, dishwasher, and microwave, along with kitchenware and a dining table for mealtime convenience. A washing machine is also provided for added convenience during your stay.

Rest comfortably in the bedrooms, furnished with fresh linens and ample wardrobe space. The bathroom features additional amenities such as bathrobes and free toiletries.

Relax in the living area, which includes a sofa, seating area, and desk for your comfort. Stay entertained with a flat-screen TV offering streaming services and satellite channels.

For those traveling with pets, rest assured that they are welcome at no extra charge. The property is also equipped with safety features including a carbon monoxide detector.

Enjoy your stay in this private apartment, situated within a detached building. Whether you're traveling with family or friends, this property offers a comfortable and convenient retreat in Lucca.

2- Casa Paolina

Piazza XX Settembre 2, Lucca

Casa Paolina provides comfortable air-conditioned apartments nestled within the historic center of Lucca, conveniently situated just a 10-minute walk from the train station. Guests can enjoy complimentary Wi-Fi access and access to a bike rental service during their stay.

The apartments feature a modern decor and are equipped with fully-equipped kitchens, allowing guests to prepare their meals at their convenience. Each apartment also includes a living area with a TV for entertainment. Depending on the layout, the apartments may offer one or two bathrooms, and some even feature a relaxing spa bath.

Positioned within the medieval city walls of Lucca, Casa Paolina Apartments offer easy access to popular attractions such as the Piazza dell'Anfiteatro and the San Martino Cathedral, both just a short stroll away.

For guests arriving by car, the apartments are conveniently located less than 2 km from the A11 motorway. Pisa Galileo Galilei Airport is also easily accessible, just a 40-minute drive from Casa Paolina.

Casa Paolina offers a range of amenities to ensure a comfortable stay for guests. These include parking facilities, with public parking available nearby (reservation may be required, charges may apply), as well as street parking options.

Each apartment is equipped with air conditioning for added comfort, along with a private bathroom for convenience. Guests traveling with pets can also request accommodation for their furry companions, with applicable charges.

The apartments feature well-equipped kitchens or kitchenettes, complete with dining tables and kitchenware, providing the convenience of preparing meals onsite. Bedrooms offer wardrobe or closet space, with some units featuring dressing rooms for added convenience.

For relaxation and entertainment, guests can enjoy the living areas with sofas and flat-screen TVs with satellite channels. Outdoor spaces such as terraces and outdoor furniture offer opportunities to unwind and enjoy the surroundings.

Additionally, guests can take advantage of wellness amenities, including massage services and hot tubs, available for an additional charge.

Other facilities and services include options for transportation, such as bicycle rental, shuttle service, and car hire, along with assistance with public transport tickets and airport shuttle services (additional charges may apply).

The property also provides reception services, including private check-in/check-out, tour desk assistance, and lockers. Babysitting/child services are available for families traveling with children, and cleaning services such as daily housekeeping and laundry can be arranged for an extra fee.

Business facilities such as fax/photocopying services are also available for guests needing to attend to work-related tasks during their stay.

Casa Paolina ensures a safe and secure environment with CCTV surveillance, smoke alarms, security alarms, and key access. The property is equipped with amenities catering to various needs, including designated smoking areas, air conditioning, heating, and allergy-free rooms.

Staff members are fluent in English and Italian, ensuring effective communication and assistance for guests throughout their stay.

3- Finca del Sol

Via San Giorgio 56, Lucca

Located in Lucca, just 300 meters from San Michele in Foro and the city center, Finca del Sol offers air-conditioned accommodations with complimentary Wi-Fi access and a shared lounge area.

Each unit at the property features a comfortable seating area, a flat-screen TV, and a private bathroom equipped with a hairdryer, bidet, and shower.

Guests staying at the apartment can indulge in a buffet or Italian-style breakfast served on-site.

Popular landmarks such as Piazza dell'Anfiteatro and Piazza Napoleone are within walking distance, with the former being 400 meters away and the latter 500 meters away from Finca del Sol. The nearest airport, Pisa International Airport, is situated 36 kilometers from the accommodation.

Conveniently located in Lucca, Finca del Sol offers a range of amenities to enhance your stay. With nearby public parking available at a surcharge, guests can easily explore the area. Complimentary WiFi access ensures you stay connected throughout your visit. Each accommodation is equipped with air conditioning for added comfort, along with a flat-screen TV for entertainment. The property also features a shared kitchen facility and a cozy seating area, providing a homely atmosphere. For guests' convenience, a tea/coffee maker is available, perfect for enjoying a hot beverage at any time. Additionally, walking tours can be arranged for an extra charge, allowing visitors to discover the local area with ease. Other services include bicycle rental, shuttle service, and an airport shuttle, all available for an additional fee. The multilingual staff at the 24-hour front desk are on hand to assist with luggage storage, tour bookings, and any queries you may have. With its commitment to providing a comfortable and convenient stay, Finca del Sol is an ideal choice for travelers exploring Lucca and its surroundings.

EXPLORING LUCCA

- Top Attractions
- Historic Sites
- Museums and Galleries
- Parks and Gardens

EXPLORING LUCCA

Top Attractions

1. Climb the Guinigi Tower

Built in the 14th and 15th centuries, the tower's origins trace back to Lucca's medieval times. It served as a defensive structure, a fortified lookout offering protection during a turbulent period. For the powerful Guinigi family, the tower's height (44.25 meters) wasn't just functional; it was a symbol of their prestige and influence within the city.

The Guinigi Tower exemplifies the local Romanesque-Gothic architectural style. Its distinctive feature is the use of red brick, giving it a warm and rustic look. Atop the tower sits a unique element – a rooftop garden featuring holm oak trees. These trees, believed to symbolize rebirth and prosperity, add a whimsical touch and contribute to the tower's iconic silhouette.

The Guinigi Tower is part of a larger complex that includes two magnificent Guinigi family mansions. These palaces, though altered over time, retain their grandeur and architectural significance. Today, one of the palaces houses the National Museum, showcasing Lucca's rich cultural heritage and offering a glimpse into the lives of its noble families.

Climbing the 233 steps of the Guinigi Tower is an experience in itself. The reward is a breathtaking panoramic view of Lucca's cityscape, enjoyed from a unique vantage point beneath the canopy of the ancient holm oak trees. This immersive experience allows visitors to appreciate not just the architectural beauty of the tower but also the charm and history of Lucca that unfolds below.

2. Anfiteatro Romano (Roman Amphitheater)

As you weave through the enchanting streets of Lucca's historic center, prepare to be surprised by the intriguing whispers of the past woven into the very fabric of the city. Amongst the captivating blend of ancient and medieval architecture, Piazza del Mercato stands out as a unique treasure trove of history, disguised as a charming square.

Unbeknownst to most, the seemingly ordinary oval shape of Piazza del Mercato holds a fascinating secret. This very spot was once the bustling heart of Lucca's Roman amphitheater, dating all the way back to the 2nd century BC! Imagine the roar of the crowd as gladiatorial contests and other spectacles unfolded within these very walls. While barbarian invasions ravaged much of the structure, the amphitheater's legacy lives on.

Look closely and you'll see the amphitheater's story etched into the very layout of the piazza and surrounding buildings. The massive stone walls, though partially destroyed, still define the oval shape. Over time, clever medieval architects incorporated the amphitheater's remnants into their designs, building houses on top of its superstructure. This ingenious strategy preserved the amphitheater's footprint within the city's urban fabric, creating a unique historical blend.

Today, Piazza del Mercato offers a captivating portal to Lucca's rich past. As you stroll through the square, admire the architectural hints of the Roman amphitheater, allowing your imagination to recreate the vibrant events that once took place here.

Piazza del Mercato isn't just about whispers of the past; it's a vibrant hub buzzing with activity throughout the year.

Immerse yourself in culture: Witness captivating street performances, browse through artisanal markets overflowing with local treasures, or participate in exciting cultural festivals. The piazza comes alive with the energy of these events, offering a window into Lucca's contemporary spirit.

A feast for the senses: Indulge in the culinary delights of Tuscany at the numerous cafes and restaurants lining the square. Savor delicious local dishes surrounded by the ancient backdrop of Lucca's historic center, creating an unforgettable dining experience.

Shopping with a twist: For those seeking unique souvenirs, browse the stalls at the occasional flea markets held in the piazza. You might just find a hidden gem or a charming piece of Lucca's history to take home.

People-watching paradise: Grab a gelato, perch yourself on a bench, and soak up the atmosphere. Watch locals going about their day, children chasing pigeons, and artists capturing the square's essence in their work.

Venturing beyond the piazza, explore the charming streets branching out from it. You might stumble upon hidden courtyards, historic churches, or quaint shops tucked away in corners. This exploration allows you to discover the hidden gems that contribute to Lucca's unique charm.

Piazza del Mercato offers a unique experience for every visitor. Whether you're a history buff yearning to connect with the past, a culture enthusiast seeking vibrant experiences, or simply a curious traveler wanting to soak up the local atmosphere, this piazza has something for everyone. So, come explore, wander, and let Lucca's history and contemporary spirit weave their magic around you.

3. Walk or Bicycle the Town Walls

Lucca's historic center isn't just a collection of charming streets and buildings; it's a fortified sanctuary embraced by a magnificent crown – the Lucca Walls. These are no ordinary walls; they are a testament to the city's rich history, strategic importance, and ongoing evolution.

Imagine towering ramparts standing guard for over 500 years! Construction began in 1504 under the watchful eyes of Flemish engineers, determined to safeguard Lucca's rectangular heart. For over four decades, they meticulously built these formidable walls, stretching 4.195 kilometers in length and reaching a height of 12 meters. At their base, an impressive thickness of 30 meters ensured Lucca's impregnability during turbulent times.

A Transformation Through Time:

Fast forward to the 19th century, and Lucca's walls undergo a fascinating metamorphosis. Maria Luigia of Bourbon, sister to Napoleon, envisioned a greener future for the city. Between 1823 and 1832, under her patronage, the once-militaristic walls blossomed into a sprawling public garden. This visionary move not only enhanced the city's aesthetics but also gifted its residents a tranquil haven.

Today, the Lucca Walls have become a beloved local landmark and a tourist magnet. Imagine yourself strolling or cycling along the tree-lined ramparts, the gentle Tuscan breeze carrying whispers of history. Below you, the old town unfolds like a living museum, adorned with terracotta rooftops, elegant palaces, and captivating churches. Each turn offers a breathtaking panorama, a postcard-perfect snapshot of Lucca's timeless beauty. Sundays come alive with a vibrant energy as locals and tourists alike gather for picnics, leisurely walks, or simply to soak in the tranquility of this unique urban oasis.

The grandeur of the Lucca Walls extends beyond the ramparts. Each of the six strategically placed gates holds a unique story. Explore the imposing Porta San Pietro on the south side, a gateway that witnessed countless travelers and dignitaries enter the city. Head north to

Porta Santa Maria, adorned with intricate Renaissance sculptures. Don't miss Porta San Donato at the west end, a powerful reminder of Lucca's medieval fortifications. These historic portals are more than just entry points; they are silent sentinels guarding the city's rich heritage.

Shop for unique treasures: Browse the vibrant antique markets, discover locally-made souvenirs, or find that perfect piece of Italian fashion.

Unwind in hidden courtyards: Seek refuge from the midday sun in a tranquil courtyard adorned with cascading flowers, a hidden gem tucked away in a quiet corner.

Lucca's walls are more than just a physical barrier; they are a symbol of the city's resilience, evolution, and enduring charm. A visit to Lucca promises a captivating journey through time, where history whispers from the ramparts, culture thrives in the streets, and the essence of Tuscany lingers in the air. So, lace up your walking shoes, rent a bike, or simply lose yourself in the enchanting embrace of Lucca's walls. This unforgettable experience awaits.

4. Cathedral

Lucca's Cathedral, also known as the Duomo di San Martino, isn't just a building; it's a captivating portal through time. Its magnificent Romanesque facade, adorned with intricate arches and sculptures, whispers tales of centuries past, inviting you to explore the artistic and spiritual treasures within.

A Walk-Through Time:
Step onto the very ground where a church has stood since the 7th century. The current cathedral, built in the 13th century, is a testament to Lucca's dedication to faith and artistry. As you approach the facade, admire the exquisite sculptures by Lombard artisans, each one a masterpiece in stone. Don't miss the main doorway, adorned with Nicola Pisano's 13th-century masterpiece depicting scenes from the life of St. Martin, the cathedral's patron saint.

A Towering Presence:
Gaze upwards at the imposing campanile, a 69-meter-tall tower constructed from light-colored travertine and brick. This iconic landmark stands as a silent guardian

over the city, offering panoramic views (for those willing to climb the stairs) that encompass Lucca's terracotta rooftops and sprawling piazzas. Look closely at the right pier of the portico – you might spot a curious labyrinth carving, potentially predating the famous Chartres maze!

A Feast for the Senses:

Step inside the cathedral and prepare to be awestruck by the artistic and architectural marvels that unfold before you. To your right, a masterpiece of Romanesque sculpture awaits: the early 13th-century stone carving depicting St. Martin and the beggar. As you explore further, admire the artistry of the pulpit by Matteo Civitali, the vibrant paintings by Doménico Ghirlandaio in the sacristy, and the breathtaking stained-glass windows in the apse, dating back to the 15th century. Keep an eye out for the captivating statue of St. John the Evangelist by Iácopo della Quercia and the stunning 1509 Madonna by Fra Bartolommeo in the adjoining Cappella del Santuario.

A Treasured Legacy:

Venture into the left transept, where you'll encounter the tomb of Ilaria del Carretto, an early 15th-century masterpiece by Iácopo della Quercia. Its delicate beauty and poignant story leave a lasting impression. But the most revered treasure of the cathedral lies ahead – the Volto Santo, a venerated wooden effigy of Christ on the Cross. Legend has it that this cedarwood carving, attributed to Nicodemus, is carried through the streets in a solemn procession every September 13th, an event deeply woven into Lucca's religious heritage.

Beyond the Walls:

For the curious explorer, the cathedral museum offers a treasure trove of medieval hymnals, intricate goldwork, and notable artworks, including a crucifix by Pisano. Here, you can delve deeper into the cathedral's rich history and gain a newfound appreciation for the artistry and faith that permeate its walls.

Your visit to the cathedral isn't complete without experiencing its unique atmosphere. Take a moment to sit in quiet contemplation, allowing the soft light filtering through the stained-glass windows to wash over you. Listen to the gentle strains of sacred music, or simply admire the intricate details of the architecture. The cathedral offers a welcome respite from the bustling city, a space for reflection and spiritual connection.

5. San Michele in Foro

San Michele in Foro, with its breathtaking façade reminiscent of a meticulously crafted wedding cake, commands attention as it graces a broad piazza in the heart of Lucca's historic center. Often mistaken for Lucca's cathedral due to its grandeur, this iconic church stands on the site of the ancient Roman forum and bears witness to centuries of architectural splendor.

Construction of San Michele spanned from the 12th to the 14th centuries, resulting in a remarkable structure adorned with a façade crafted from intricately carved and inlaid marble. The façade, reminiscent of a layered masterpiece, showcases four tiers of meticulously worked pillars, with each layer boasting a unique design seldom repeated. Dominating the ensemble is a larger-than-life-size statue of Archangel Michael, imparting a sense of grandeur and spirituality.

Stepping inside, visitors are transported back in time to experience the Romanesque charm of the interior. Notable highlights include the terra-cotta Madonna and Child sculpture by Andrea della Robbia, adding a touch of Renaissance elegance to the sacred space. In the left transept, visitors can admire a 15th-century painted panel depicting saints Roch, Sebastian, Jerome, and Helen, showcasing the exquisite craftsmanship of Filippo Lippi, one of the Renaissance masters.

Addressed at Piazza San Michele, Lucca, this architectural marvel invites tourists to marvel at its timeless beauty and immerse themselves in the rich history and artistic heritage of Lucca. Whether admiring the intricacies of its façade, exploring its Romanesque interior, or simply basking in the tranquil atmosphere of the surrounding piazza, San Michele in Foro offers a captivating experience for visitors of all ages.

6. San Frediano

As you explore Lucca's enchanting streets, don't miss the captivating Basilica of San Frediano, a treasure trove of history and artistic wonder. Dedicated to the revered 6th-century Bishop Saint Frediano, this basilica boasts a unique story, architectural intrigue, and artistic delights waiting to be discovered.

A Curious Reversal:

Step back in time to the 12th century and imagine the construction of San Frediano. Initially built with a traditional east-facing chancel, the church underwent a fascinating transformation in the 13th century. As Lucca's city walls rose, strategically blocking the original eastern entrance, the builders embarked on a bold project. They flipped the script! A new apse with the altar was constructed on the west end, essentially reversing the church's orientation. This unique solution ensured the main entrance wouldn't be overshadowed by the imposing city walls.

A Masterpiece on Display:

Look skyward and marvel at the magnificent facade. Unlike most Tuscan churches, San Frediano boasts a stunning Italo-Byzantine mosaic masterpiece. Created by Berlinghiero Berlinghieri, this colossal artwork depicts Christ flanked by angels, with the 12 Apostles gazing upwards in reverence. It's a rare sight in Tuscany, with only one other church (San Miniato al Monte in Florence) sharing this unique decorative feature.

A Journey Through Time:

Step inside the basilica and embark on a captivating journey. The interior, divided into three aisles with majestic columns, offers a harmonious blend of Romanesque and Gothic styles. As you explore, keep an eye out for these hidden gems:

The 12th-century Font: In the first chapel on the right, admire a beautifully restored mid-12th-century font. Imagine the countless baptisms that have taken place here over the centuries.

Cappella Trenta: The fourth chapel on the left, adorned with the name "Cappella Trenta" (Chapel of Thirty), boasts a treasure trove of artistic mastery. Be mesmerized by the richly decorated Gothic marble polyptych, featuring captivating 15th-century bas-reliefs by the renowned sculptor Iácopo della Quercia. The Madonna and Child with Saints scene is a testament to his artistry.

Beyond the Basilica:
A visit to San Frediano isn't just about the church itself. Take some time to explore the charming Piazza San Frediano, the square where the basilica stands. Here, you can:

Relax in a cafe: Sip on a cup of espresso and soak in the local atmosphere. People-watching and enjoying the gentle pace of life are perfect ways to unwind after exploring the basilica.

Visit nearby attractions: Lucca is brimming with hidden gems. Explore the Guinigi Tower with its rooftop garden, or delve into the rich collections at the National Museum, located in the former Guinigi Palace complex.

7. Stroll through Piazza Napoleone

Lucca's main square, Piazza Napoleone, boasts an array of architectural treasures that showcase the city's rich history and cultural heritage. On the west side stands the imposing facade of the Palazzo della Provincia, a testament to Renaissance grandeur. Constructed from 1578 onwards, this majestic building replaced an earlier Palazzo and serves as a prominent landmark in the square.

Adjacent to the Palazzo della Provincia, towards the southwest, stands the Church of San Romano, a historic gem erected by the Dominicans in 1280. While the exterior facade remains unfinished, the church houses the Tomb of St. Romanus, a notable artistic and religious treasure dating back to 1490.

Near the northeast corner of Piazza Napoleone, visitors will discover the charming 12th-century church of San Giusto, characterized by its austere facade crafted from sandstone and adorned with bands of marble. Despite its modest exterior, the church boasts a lavishly decorated main doorway that captivates with its intricate details.

Inside, the interior underwent a Baroque remodeling in the mid-17th century, offering a glimpse into the evolving architectural styles that have shaped Lucca over the centuries.

These architectural landmarks not only enhance the beauty of Piazza Napoleone but also serve as poignant reminders of Lucca's rich religious and cultural heritage. Whether admiring the Renaissance elegance of the Palazzo della Provincia or exploring the historic sanctuaries of San Romano and San Giusto, visitors to Piazza Napoleone are treated to a captivating journey through time.

8. Linger in the Garden at Palazzo Pfanner-Controni

The Palazzo Pfanner-Controni, situated just within the walls on the north side of Lucca's historic old town, stands as a remarkable example of Renaissance architecture, having been erected in 1667. Its distinctive feature is the elegant two-story loggia with a staircase, exuding a sense of harmony and sophistication characteristic of the period.

A major highlight of the Palazzo Pfanner-Controni is its stunning Baroque Garden, an exquisite addition dating back to the 17th century and attributed to the renowned architect Filippo Juvarra, known for his significant contributions to Turin's architectural landscape. Despite its relatively modest size, the garden boasts a remarkable array of features, including monumental statuary, exotic trees, meticulously manicured hedges, a lemon house, a tranquil pool, and a captivating fountain. The meticulous arrangement of these elements creates an illusion of spaciousness, enhancing the garden's allure.

Stepping inside the palazzo, visitors are treated to a visual feast of 18th-century frescoes adorning the walls, crafted by the skilled artist Pietro Paolo Scorsini. Additionally, the palazzo houses a notable collection of medical implements, offering insight into the history of medicine and healthcare.

The Palazzo Pfanner-Controni is a captivating destination that seamlessly blends architectural splendor with natural beauty, inviting visitors to immerse themselves in the timeless charm of Lucca's cultural heritage. Whether exploring the graceful loggia, strolling through the enchanting garden, or marveling at the artistic treasures within the palazzo, a visit to this historic landmark promises an unforgettable experience.

(Address: Via degli Asili 33, Lucca)

Historic Sites

1. Le Mura Di Lucca

Lucca's monumental walls, erected during the 16th and 17th centuries, stand as an enduring testament to the city's rich history and strategic significance. Remarkably well-preserved, these imposing fortifications stretch approximately 4 kilometers in length and soar to a height of twelve meters. Thanks to Lucca's prolonged periods of tranquility and peace, the walls have retained their structural integrity over the centuries.

Atop the ramparts lies a picturesque tree-lined footpath, offering panoramic vistas of the historic centro storico (old town) and the majestic Apuane Alps beyond. This elevated pathway serves as a beloved gathering spot for locals engaging in the traditional evening stroll known as the passeggiata. Whether on foot, bicycle, or inline skates, residents and visitors alike relish the opportunity to leisurely traverse this scenic route, soaking in the enchanting ambiance of Lucca's architectural marvels and natural beauty.

Along the way, several of the eleven bastions dotting the walls, including Baluardo San Regolo, Baluardo San Salvatore, and Baluardo Santa Croce, bustle with activity. Here, children frolic in designated play areas equipped with playgrounds, swings, and picnic tables nestled beneath the sheltering canopy of plane trees. Meanwhile, older youths engage in spirited games of soccer on the expansive green lawns of Baluardo San Donato, infusing the surroundings with energy and vitality.

The walls of Lucca not only serve as a tangible link to the city's storied past but also as a vibrant hub of community life, where generations come together to enjoy leisurely pursuits and savor the simple joys of camaraderie amidst breathtaking surroundings.

Visiting Le Mura Di Lucca comes with some essential travel tips to ensure a smooth experience. From January 1 to March 20 and from November 5 to December 31, access is available by appointment only, so it's advisable to plan your visit accordingly.

When it comes to entrance ticket details, there are various options to consider. For the Botanical Garden, the full price ranges from €3.00 for individuals aged 14 to 65 years. Reduced admission applies to children aged 6 to 14 and individuals over 65. Groups of over 10 persons organized with a tour guide can avail themselves of a reduced rate of €2.00. For a comprehensive experience, a combined ticket for the entire Botanical Gardens, Guinigi Tower, and Clock Tower is available for €6.00.

Additionally, there are special rates for specific groups, such as the Tower of the Hours, where groups over 10 people organized with a tour guide, individuals over 65, and children from 6 to 14 years old can access it for €5.00. Children under 6 years old, disabled individuals with an escort, and schools from the town of Lucca enjoy free admission. Municipal schools can also arrange visits for an extra fee of €30.00 per class, while Lucca citizens can obtain a special card for €20.00.

Reaching Le Mura Di Lucca is convenient by bus, offering accessibility to a wide range of visitors. After exploring the walls, visitors can indulge in culinary delights at nearby restaurants such as Albergo Celide and Gli Orti di Via Elisa, rounding off their experience with a satisfying meal.

2. San Michele In Foro

Address: Piazza San Michele, 55100 Lucca, Italy
Timings: 09:00 am - 06:00 pm
Phone: 390-583583150
Time Required: 01:00 Hrs

San Michele In Foro holds a significant historical legacy, dating back to its mention in 795 AD with the title "ad foro," indicating its location within the ancient Roman forum. Positioned at the heart of the ancient Roman town, the church stands as a basilica with three aisles, a transept, and a semicircular apse. Its architectural features include arches supported by monolithic pillars and barrel vaults with lunettes covering the entire structure. The bell tower rises above the southern transept, adding to its distinctive silhouette. The exterior boasts a remarkable façade adorned with intricate ribbed and sculpted designs, constructed mainly from perfectly squared limestone blocks.

For travelers visiting San Michele In Foro, maintaining the peaceful ambiance of this religious site is essential. Modest dressing is recommended out of respect for the sacred atmosphere, and photography without prior permission is prohibited to preserve the sanctity of the space.

Accessing San Michele In Foro is convenient via bus transportation, offering easy reach for visitors eager to explore its historical significance. After immersing oneself in the rich heritage of the church, nearby restaurants like La Buca di Sant'Antonio and Ristorante Piccolo Mondo provide opportunities to savor local culinary delights, complementing the cultural experience with culinary indulgence.

3. Ortobotanico Di Lucca

Address: Via del Giardino Botanico, 14, 55100 Lucca, Ital

Timings: 09:30 am - 11:59 pm

Phone: 390-583442160

Ticket Price: 3 EUR

Time Required: 02:00 Hrs

The Ortobotanico Di Lucca is a botanical garden with a rich history, initially established alongside a laboratory for Physics and an observatory for Astronomy. It boasts a diverse collection of two hundred plant species, including early-flowering azaleas, camellias, and rhododendrons. Acquired by the City of Lucca in 1920, the garden was transformed into a public space, preserving its botanical heritage for the enjoyment of visitors.

Visitors to the Ortobotanico Di Lucca will encounter various decorative elements that enhance the garden's charm and historical significance. Ceramic medallions depict key milestones in the garden's history, while ornamental features like a gate adorned with relief laurel leaves and sculpted lions add to its allure. A terracotta sphinx and a large pumpkin accentuate the octagonal pool, which nurtures aquatic plants, while Virginia cypresses provide a picturesque backdrop near the lake.

Entrance to the Ortobotanico Di Lucca is available at a reduced fee of 2.00 Euros, allowing visitors to immerse themselves in the botanical wonders within. Accessible by bus, reaching the garden is convenient for travelers exploring Lucca's cultural and natural attractions. After a delightful stroll through the botanical wonders, nearby restaurants such as Gli Orti di Via Elisa and Albergo Celide offer opportunities to savor delectable cuisine, completing a memorable day in Lucca.

4. Via Fillungo

Address: Etnea Street, Lucca, Italy

Timings: 24-hrs

Via Fillungo, named after Garfagnana's Fillongo Castle, offers a captivating journey through the historic charm of old Lucca. A leisurely stroll along this street provides a wonderful opportunity to immerse oneself in the city's rich heritage. While you may choose not to enter every notable establishment, simply observing them from the outside adds to the experience. Here are some highlights to explore along Via Fillungo:

Palazzo Manzi: A distinguished patrician residence dating back to the 15th century, Palazzo Manzi showcases exquisite architectural features and historical significance.

Church of San Cristoforo: This austere-faced church, originating from the 11th century, serves as a restored exhibition space for various events and concerts, offering a glimpse into Lucca's religious and cultural heritage.

Accademia dei Collegati: Home to a prestigious theater, the Accademia dei Collegati epitomizes Lucca's vibrant performing arts scene and hosts a range of captivating performances.

Clock Tower of Lucida Mansi: A notable landmark along Via Fillungo, the Clock Tower of Lucida Mansi adds to the street's allure with its distinctive architecture and historical significance.

When exploring Via Fillungo, keep in mind the following travel tips:

The theater may be closed for safety reasons but can still be admired from the outside.

Separate entry fees may apply for attractions such as Palazzo Manzi and the clock tower.

Reaching Via Fillungo is convenient via bus, allowing visitors easy access to this iconic street. After a delightful exploration, nearby restaurants like Eno Ristorante Micheloni and Casina delle Rose offer opportunities to indulge in authentic Tuscan cuisine, completing a memorable day in Lucca.

5. Casa Di Puccini

Address: Corte San Lorenzo 9, 55100 Lucca (LU), Italy
Timings: 10:00 am - 06:00 pm
Phone: 390-583584028
Ticket Price: 3 EUR
Time Required: 01:00 Hrs

Casa di Puccini holds a special place in Lucca's cultural heritage as the birthplace and residence of the world-renowned artist and performer, Giacomo Puccini, for 22 years. Situated in Corte San Lorenzo, this historic house is now a museum managed by the Giacomo Puccini Foundation in Lucca, offering visitors a glimpse into the life and work of the celebrated composer.

The museum houses a fascinating collection of personal items, including furniture, awards bestowed upon the maestro, and notable compositions such as the Messa a Quattro voci (1880) and Il Capriccio Sinfonico (1883). Additionally, Casa di Puccini features a rich archive of letters exchanged between Giacomo Puccini, his wife Elvira, his son Antonio, and his publisher Giulio Ricordi, providing insight into their personal and professional lives.

For those interested in exploring Casa di Puccini, here are some important details:

Entrance Ticket Details: Reduced admission fee of 2.00 Euros is available, and entry is free on November 29th and December 22nd.

How to Reach Casa Di Puccini: Accessible by bus, Casa di Puccini is conveniently located in Lucca's city center, making it easily accessible to visitors.

After a captivating visit to Casa di Puccini, nearby restaurants such as La Buca di Sant'Antonio and Puccini offer opportunities to savor authentic Tuscan cuisine, adding to the cultural experience of exploring Lucca's musical heritage.

Top of Form

6. Torre Delle Ore

Address: Via dell'Arancio, Lucca, Italy

Timings: 10:30 am - 06:30 pm

Phone: 390-583316846

Ticket Price: 3 EUR

Time Required: 01:00 Hrs

Standing tall as the highest tower overlooking the city of Lucca, the Torre delle Ore traces its construction back to the 14th century. Rising to a height of 164 meters, this tower stands as a resilient survivor among the city's once plentiful 130 towers. Originally built as part of a home for a wealthy family, the tower served both protective and symbolic purposes, representing power and affluence.

One of the tower's distinctive features is its ancient clock mechanism, which is still manually wound by hand. Visitors are treated to the mesmerizing sight of the intricate wheels and gears in motion when the bells chime. Climbing the tower is an unforgettable experience, with 207 well-maintained wooden stairs leading to the top. From there, visitors can marvel at the breathtaking panoramic views of Lucca and capture cherished memories through photographs.

Here are some travel tips for visiting the Torre delle Ore:

The staircase is narrow and steep, so it may pose challenges for elderly visitors.

Avoid standing near the tower bells when they strike on the hour, as the noise can be very loud.

For those planning to visit, here are the entrance ticket details:

Ticket Prices: 2.50 Euros (discounted for servicemen, children under 10, groups of 20 or more, students, and individuals over 65); 6.50 Euros for a combined ticket to access both the Torre delle Ore and Torre Guinigi.

To reach the Torre delle Ore, visitors can easily access it by bus. The tower's address is Via dell'Arancio in Lucca, and it can be contacted at +390-583316846. The tower is open from 10:30 am to 06:30 pm, with the best time to visit between 02:00 pm and 06:00 pm. Typically, a visit to the tower lasts approximately one hour.

7. Museo Nazionale Di Palazzo Mansi

Situated in Lucca's city center, Palazzo Mansi is a significant national gallery of art dating back to the 16th century. Originally purchased by the Mansi family in 1616, the palace underwent internal restructuring in the Baroque style, contrasting with its austere exterior features. The two wings added in the 19th century feature a staircase with a single ramp leading to the main floor, offering views of the garden from a loggia.

Since the late 20th century, the State has recovered the original furnishings, frescoes, and tapestries, restoring the luxury of this historic building. Noteworthy are the frescoes adorning the ceilings and the Bridal Chamber with its original alcove and embroidered silk fabrics from the 18th century.

The museum showcases works by 19th-century artists such as Pompeo Batoni, Bernardino Nocchi, and Stefano Tofanelli. Additionally, it features a collection of ancient textiles and everyday life objects, offering insight into Lucca's textile production.

The art gallery displays paintings donated by Grand Duke Leopold II of Habsburg-Lorraine, including works by Tintoretto, Ghirlandaio, Veronese, Titian, Guido Reni, and Domenichino.

Here are some details for visiting Museo Nazionale di Palazzo Mansi:

- ❖ Entrance Ticket: Concessions €2.00; Cumulative ticket for both National Museums €6.50 (concessions €3.25); free admission for children under 18 and seniors over 65.
- ❖ Wait time for ticket purchase: approximately 5 minutes.
- ❖ Opening Hours: Last admission at 07:00 pm.
- ❖ To reach the museum, visitors can use the bus.
- ❖ Address: Via Galli Tassi, 43, 55100 Lucca, Italy
- ❖ Contact Number: +390-58355570
- ❖ Timing: 08:30 am - 07:30 pm
- ❖ Price: 4 EUR
- ❖ Best Time to Visit: 10:00 am - 05:00 pm
- ❖ Time Required: Approximately 2 hours.

8. Roman Amphitheatre Or Piazza Anfiteatro

Constructed in the second half of the 1st century A.D., the Roman amphitheatre in Lucca was initially designed to host gladiatorial shows and games. Over the centuries, it underwent multiple renovations and rebuilds, with evidence of these changes discovered during 19th-century excavations. Notable archaeological finds include coins from the reign of Emperor Claudius and inscriptions indicating significant donations.

During the 19th century, architect Lorenzo Nottolini led a project to demolish the buildings within the ancient arena, resulting in the creation of the present-day Piazza dell'Anfiteatro. The elliptical shape of the square closely corresponds to the area of the ancient arena, providing visitors with a sense of its original volume and outline. Along the outer perimeter, remnants of the original walls can be seen, particularly along Via dell'Anfiteatro.

Here are some travel tips for visiting the Roman Amphitheatre or Piazza dell'Anfiteatro:

- Guided tours are available for a deeper understanding of the site's history.
- To reach the site, visitors can use the bus.
- Address: Piazza dell'Anfiteatro, 55100 Lucca, Italy
- Contact Number: +39-05834422
- Timing: Open 24 hours
- Best Time to Visit: 10:00 am - 06:00 pm
- Time Required: Approximately 2 hours.

Museums and Galleries

1. Pinacoteca Palazzo Mansi

Originally a beautiful building, the Pinacoteca Palazzo Mansi later came under the ownership of the State, which transformed it into a museum. Dating back to the 16th century, it was later acquired by the Mansi family and adorned in Baroque style. Visitors can admire artworks from the 19th century as well as pieces from Flemish, Roman, and Tuscan schools. Intact frames and models representing clothing from the era are also of interest.

Address: Via Galli Tassi, 43

Telephone: +39 0583 461

2. Giacomo Puccini's Birthplace Museum

The birthplace of renowned composer Giacomo Puccini, this museum reopened on September 13, 2011. Puccini, born here on December 22, 1858, spent most of his formative years in this house. The museum, now a popular tourist destination, offers guided tours covering the artist's life from birth to his final masterpiece, Turandot. Visitors can view family portraits, musician portraits, letters, and the famous Steinway piano on which Turandot was composed in Viareggio.

3. National Museum of Villa Guinigi

Restored after World War II, this house became a museum in 1924 and was later transformed into the National Museum. The museum showcases artistic and historical artifacts, including prehistoric carvings and Baroque paintings. Of scientific interest are eighteenth- and nineteenth-century measuring instruments.

Address: Via della Quarquonia

4. Cathedral Museum

Arranged chronologically, the Cathedral Museum allows visitors to follow a path through history. Exhibits include the ivory diptych of Areobindo, a copper box depicting the martyrdom of Becket, and paintings by Vincenzo Frediani and Francesco Marti Silver.

5. Botanical Garden

Established in 1820 during the reign of Duchess Maria Luisa of Bourbon, the Lucca Botanical Garden is one of the oldest still-active botanical gardens. Divided into different sections, it offers a chance to observe local fauna, medicinal plants, and various species of intertropical plants. Of particular interest is the Cedar of Lebanon, planted in 1822 by Paul Foxes, the garden's first director.

6. Archaeological Museum in the Garfagnana

Restored after severe bombing in World War II, this museum features two sections. The first focuses on the Mesolithic period and archaeological excavations of that era, while the second is dedicated to the Ligurian Apuan people and their customs around the third century BC when they settled in Garfagnana.

7. Civic Museum of Villa Paolina

Once the summer residence of Paolina Bonaparte, this museum offers insights into a woman's private life. Over the years, it has served various purposes, from a public school to a meeting place for education, until it was heavily damaged during World War II.

8. Historical Museum of the Resistance

Located in St. Anna di Stazzema, an important site of Italian resistance, this museum provides a glimpse into the events of that era. Drawing on historical records, images, and testimonies, it showcases the active role of Versilia in the fight for liberation.

Parks and Gardens

1. Urban wall park

The 4-kilometer-long towering walls encompassing the city also serve as a botanical path, meandering amidst the trees lining the curtains and bastions.

Native species such as poplars, elms, and holm oaks, found on the oldest bastions or in areas untouched by change, coexist with linden trees, plane trees, lyriodendrons, oaks, hackberry trees, and unique specimens like an imposing red beech and a rare South American cypress. A grove of hornbeams, holm oaks in a "Ragnaia" wood, catalpas, and a diverse collection of magnolias, whose spring blooms are eagerly awaited by strollers, embellish the path leading down from the walls to Corso Garibaldi.

Maria Luisa di Borbone initiated the transformation of the walls into a vast city park, designed "for the delight and leisure of citizens." She expanded the promenade, adorned the gardens above the bulwarks, and created shaded areas with plane trees and other local and exotic tree species.

In the 19th century, the former military fortifications of the city walls were repurposed into a distinctive monumental park, rising above the city as a symbol of peace, civilization, and hospitality.

The basements of the ramparts, meticulously restored and open to visitors, serve as unconventional venues for permanent art exhibitions, concerts, theater performances, and sporting events. The barracks and castles above the access gates, once housing soldiers, now host small city museums, restaurants, and cultural foundations.

In addition to the grand original entrance gates, pedestrian exits have been added, providing access from passages that were once clandestine, still retaining their old-world charm and allure.

The curtains, equivalent in length to a marathon, are favored by locals for relaxation, leisurely strolls, and sports activities. Botanical enthusiasts appreciate wandering among elms, plane trees, lyriodendrons, tulip trees, and various other species. For those inclined towards fitness, the locals engage in a "tour of the walls" either early in the morning or at sunset, jogging along the tree-lined avenues. Every Saturday morning, starting at 9:00 am from Piazzale Vittorio Emanuele, the ParkRun Mura di Lucca is organized, offering participants a chance to race against time and set personal records.

2. Aqueduct Park

From the valley temple, which houses the settling tank, a pathway winds along the aqueduct leading up to Mount Pisano, traversing the countryside south of Lucca. Along the route, it crosses the Ozzeri and Rogio canals and passes through the Verciano wood, a natural alder forest populated with willows and elms, representing one of the few remaining spontaneous woodlands in the plain of Lucca.

Behind Lucca's railway station lies the beginning—or rather, the end—of the Nottolini aqueduct, which extends underground from this point to the city center, supplying excellent drinking water to the historic center's fountains. Architect Nottolini deliberately chose not to interfere with the imposing Renaissance walls, thus halting the aqueduct's arches shortly before reaching them.

A total of 413 arches, a countryside monument, stretch for approximately three kilometers before reaching the slopes of Mount Pisano. Here, another small temple-cistern marks the spot where the aqueduct once again descends underground, making its way through the woodland until it reaches the springs area. A small bridge near the springs features an inscription commemorating the completion of the works in 1836, and their patron, Carlo Ludovico di Borbone. Locals fondly refer to this site as "the golden words." The water from these springs, considered one of the finest mineral waters in the region, is preferred by many locals over bottled water.

For those who have traveled the path in reverse, starting from the sources and ending in Lucca's historic center, a brief tour of the city's fountains is a fitting conclusion to the journey. Notable fountains include the low basin surrounded by pillars in Piazza Antelminelli, the elegant Naiade fountain in Piazza del Salvatore, and the two fountains along Via dei Fossi, designed by Lorenzo Nottolini himself.

DINING AND NIGHTLIFE

- Traditional Tuscan Cuisine
- Local Restaurants and Cafés
- Wine Bars and Pubs
- Evening Entertainment

DINING AND NIGHTLIFE

Traditional Tuscan Cuisine

Traditional Tuscan Pasta Dishes

Tuscan cuisine offers a delightful array of pasta dishes, showcasing the region's rich culinary heritage. Here are some traditional Tuscan pasta dishes featuring meat, fish, and vegetarian options:

Tordelli Lucchesi (meat): Tordelli is a beloved dish from Lucca, featuring crescent-shaped filled pasta. The dough is stuffed with a flavorful mixture of stale Tuscan bread, salt, minced beef and pork, and spices, then served with a rich meat ragu sauce. There's also a variation from Versilia that includes chard in the filling.

Pici all'aglione (vegan): Pici is a rustic pasta resembling thick spaghetti, made simply with water and flour. Originating from Val di Chiana and Val d'Orcia, it's paired with aglione sauce made from a unique garlic variety grown in southern Tuscany, along with olive oil, tomatoes, and a hint of chili pepper, resulting in a robust yet straightforward flavor.

Pappardelle al ragù di cinghiale (game): This dish hails from Maremma in South Tuscany and features pappardelle, long handmade pasta ideal for capturing sauce. The ragu, made with wild boar meat, imparts a distinctive, slightly wild flavor. Slow-cooked for hours, the ragu tenderizes the meat and infuses it with rich flavors.

Spaghetti alle arselle (fish): A specialty of Versilia, this seafood pasta stars arselle, small mollusks akin to clams but smaller, found along the sandy beaches of the region. The clams are cooked with olive oil, garlic, chili, and sometimes cherry tomatoes, then tossed with spaghetti, emphasizing the importance of high-quality shellfish for optimal taste.

Gnudi (vegetarian): Gnudi, meaning "naked" in Tuscan dialect, are essentially "naked ravioli" made from spinach, eggs, Parmesan, and ricotta, without the pasta covering. Cooked in water, they are then sautéed in butter and sage before serving, often topped with a sprinkle of Parmesan.

Testaroli (vegetarian): Originating from Lunigiana, Testaroli are crepe-like pasta made from soft wheat flour, water, and salt. Once cooked, they're cut into diamond shapes and served with oil, basil, and cheese, or sometimes paired with Genoese pesto for a flavorful vegetarian option.

These traditional Tuscan pasta dishes offer a delicious taste of the region's diverse culinary traditions, from hearty meat sauces to fresh seafood and vegetarian delights.

Tuscan Meat and Game Dishes

Tuscan cuisine is renowned for its hearty meat and game dishes, showcasing the region's rich culinary heritage. Here are some traditional Tuscan meat and game dishes that are beloved classics:

Crostini Neri: These classic Tuscan appetizers feature a spread of chicken liver pate cooked with sautéed onion, vin santo, sage, bay leaf, capers, and anchovies, served on toasted slices of Tuscan bread.

Peposo dell'Impruneta: A traditional Tuscan recipe from Impruneta, this spicy and tender stew features veal muscle slow-cooked in Chianti red wine and seasoned with copious amounts of black peppercorns.

Tonno del Chianti: Despite its name, this dish from Chianti is made with pork loin slices purged in salt for three days, then slow-cooked in white wine, herbs, and spices for about five hours until tender. It is often served with cannellini beans and fresh onion.

Scottiglia: Originating from Maremma, this meat stew features a combination of high-quality meats such as chicken, beef, turkey, lamb, pork, and sometimes game, slow-cooked in red wine, tomatoes, herbs, and spices.

Coniglio alla Cacciatora: Also known as stewed rabbit, this dish features rabbit slow-cooked in tomato sauce and olives, resulting in tender meat and a flavorful sauce.

Cinghiale in Umido: A beloved classic in Tuscan cuisine, this stewed wild boar recipe requires marinating the meat in red wine with herbs and spices for several hours before slow-cooking it with tomato sauce.

Lampredotto: A historical offal dish and a typical Florentine Street food, lampredotto is veal abomasum boiled in vegetable broth, then sliced and often served in a bun with salsa verde.

Bistecca alla Fiorentina: A hallmark of Florentine tradition, this T-bone steak is aged for at least 20 days, grilled to perfection, and served rare to preserve its tender texture and rich flavor.

These Tuscan meat and game dishes exemplify the region's culinary excellence and are cherished by locals and visitors alike for their robust flavors and comforting appeal.

Tuscan Fish and Seafood Dishes

Tuscan cuisine offers a delightful array of fish and seafood dishes, particularly from coastal regions like Livorno, Viareggio, and Elba Island. Here are some traditional Tuscan fish and seafood dishes worth exploring:

Cacciucco alla Livornese e alla Viareggina: Cacciucco, originating from Livorno, is a hearty fish stew made with various types of fish, mussels, and a rich sauce of celery, carrots, onions, tomatoes, parsley, chili pepper, and red wine. It's traditionally served with toasted garlicky bread. Cacciucco alla Viareggina, typical of Viareggio, features filleted fish and subtler flavors.

Stoccafisso all'Elbana (o Riese): This traditional dish from Rio Marina on Elba Island consists of stockfish cooked with oil, onion, chili pepper, white wine, anchovies, potatoes, cherry tomatoes, black olives, pine nuts, and capers, reflecting the culinary heritage of local sailors and their families.

Acciughe alla Povera: A classic appetizer from coastal areas like Livorno, Pisa, and Viareggio, Acciughe alla Povera features marinated anchovies prepared simply with vinegar, oil, onions, chili pepper, and anchovies, highlighting the region's coastal flavors in a humble yet delicious manner.

Triglie alla Livornese: Triglie, or mullets, alla Livornese is a quick and flavorful dish where mullets are cooked whole in a pan with oil, sautéed garlic, parsley, and tomato sauce, resulting in a simple yet delightful seafood entree.

These Tuscan fish and seafood dishes showcase the region's culinary diversity and are cherished for their rich flavors and cultural significance. Whether enjoyed in a seaside trattoria or prepared at home, they offer a taste of Tuscany's coastal heritage.

Top of Form

Tuscan Soups, Sides, Vegetarian and Vegan Dishes

Tuscan cuisine offers a delightful array of soups, sides, and vegetarian and vegan dishes, showcasing the region's rich culinary heritage. Here are some traditional Tuscan dishes worth savoring:

Pappa al Pomodoro: This bread and tomato-based soup is a Tuscan classic, perfect for using up stale bread. Made with Tuscan unsalted bread, peeled tomatoes, garlic, basil, and extra virgin olive oil, it's a comforting dish served hot in winter or at room temperature in summer.

Garmugia: Originating from the Lucchese nobility, Garmugia is a springtime soup featuring fresh seasonal vegetables like broad beans, peas, spring onions, asparagus, and artichokes, combined with minced meat and bacon for a flavorful celebration of spring.

Ribollita: A hearty bread and vegetable soup, Ribollita is a Tuscan staple made with black cabbage, savoy cabbage, beans, and stale bread. Traditionally prepared by boiling leftovers several times, it's a comforting dish perfect for colder days.

Farinata: Similar to Ribollita, Farinata is a soup made with black cabbage, cornmeal (replacing bread), and beans. It can be served as a soup or thickened and cut into slices, making it versatile and delicious.

Acquacotta: Hailing from Maremma, Acquacotta is a simple yet flavorful soup made with water, stale bread, onions, and herbs. It's typically enriched with peeled tomatoes, celery, an egg, and aged pecorino cheese for added richness.

Zuppa di Farro alla Lucchese: Spelt soup is a beloved dish in Lucca, featuring Borlotti beans, spelt, fried lard or pork rind, garlic, onions, sage, and rosemary. It's a hearty and satisfying soup often served with a drizzle of olive oil.

Panzanella: A refreshing bread salad, Panzanella is made with stale Tuscan bread soaked in water and vinegar, tomatoes, red onions, and a variety of fresh vegetables like cucumbers or celery. It's a perfect summer dish bursting with flavors.

Cecina o Torta di Ceci: Cecina is a thin chickpea-based omelette, served sliced with plenty of pepper. Made with chickpea flour, water, salt, and olive oil, it's cooked on a cast iron plate and enjoyed hot. Known as "Torta" in Livorno, it's a simple and delicious vegan dish.

Stringhe in Umido: Stringhe, a type of elongated green bean, are slow-cooked in tomato sauce with garlic, sage, and thyme, resulting in a flavorful and unique dish typical of Lucca.

These Tuscan soups, sides, and vegetarian and vegan dishes highlight the region's culinary traditions and are cherished for their simplicity and robust flavors. Whether enjoyed as a comforting soup or a refreshing salad, they offer a taste of Tuscany's diverse and vibrant food culture.

Traditional Tuscan Sweets

Tuscan sweets offer a delightful blend of flavors and textures, often rooted in the region's rich culinary heritage. Here are some traditional Tuscan desserts worth indulging in:

Cantucci e Vin Santo: These almond biscuits are crunchy on the outside and crumbly on the inside, perfect for dipping into Vin Santo, a sweet Tuscan wine. Cantucci e Vin Santo is a classic Tuscan dessert enjoyed on special occasions and celebrations.

Castagnaccio e Necci: Made with chestnut flour, castagnaccio is a baked dessert flavored with rosemary, pine nuts, and raisins, often served with fresh ricotta. Necci are chestnut flour crepes filled with ricotta or Nutella, offering a delightful combination of flavors.

Ricciarelli: Originating from Siena, ricciarelli are soft almond biscuits made with sugar and egg whites, often enjoyed during the Christmas period. These sweet treats are shaped like small loaves and dusted generously with icing sugar.

Panforte e Panpepato: Another specialty from Siena, panforte is an oven-baked dessert made with almonds, candied fruit, sugar, and honey, with a wafer sheet at the base. Panpepato, a variant of panforte, includes cocoa and pepper for added depth of flavor.

Buccellato Lucchese: This sweet bread from Lucca is flavored with aniseed and raisins, offering a delightful treat for breakfast or dessert. With its glossy brown exterior, buccellato is often enjoyed with Vin Santo or soaked in milk.

Cenci: These Tuscan carnival sweets, also known as "tea sheets," are made from a simple dough of flour, eggs, and sugar. Cut into rectangular shapes, fried, and dusted with powdered sugar, cenci are a delicious indulgence during the festive season.

Treat yourself to these traditional Tuscan sweets for a taste of the region's culinary delights and time-honored recipes. Whether enjoyed with a glass of wine or as a sweet ending to a meal, these desserts showcase the rich flavors and traditions of Tuscany.

Local Restaurants and Cafés

1. Gatta Ci Cova

Nestled near Porta Elisa, Gatta Ci Cova offers a small and cozy dining experience with modern decor that strikes a balance between elegance and simplicity. The furnishings are functional yet tastefully designed, adding to the inviting ambiance. Guests can expect excellent service from the attentive staff, who go above and beyond to ensure a comfortable dining experience. The atmosphere is youthful and vibrant, making it an ideal spot for a relaxed meal. Food quality is consistently high, with each dish meticulously prepared and well-presented. The restaurant boasts a wide and impressive selection of wines to complement the delicious cuisine. Despite its upscale vibe, Gatta Ci Cova remains affordable, making it a great value for money destination in Lucca

Address: Via Nicola Barbantini, 338 - close to the stadium, Porta Elisa

Telephone: +39 0583 496795

2. L'Imbuto

At L'Imbuto, the chef's creativity takes center stage, promising an unforgettable culinary journey. Guests are invited to select their preferred menu type and then sit back to savor each surprising and inventive dish crafted by the chef. The dining experience is truly outstanding, with delectable food paired perfectly with exceptional wines. Every plate is presented with artistic flair, showcasing the chef's imagination and attention to detail. You may find yourself hesitant to disturb such culinary masterpieces as you indulge in their flavors. Located within the Lucca Center of Contemporary Art, housed in the historic Boccella Palace near Piazza Anfiteatro, the restaurant offers a convenient and culturally rich setting for diners to enjoy their meal.

Via della Fratta 36 -Telephone: +390583491280

Closed on Mondays

3. Trattoria da Giulio

Trattoria da Giulio offers an authentic taste of Tuscan cuisine at affordable prices. Their dishes are straightforward yet embody the essence of traditional Tuscan cooking. While the menu boasts an excellent selection, it's the classics that steal the show: from comforting tortellini in brodo to hearty pasta with ragù, tripe, ravioli, and sausages with beans. Be sure to inquire about the daily specials for a delightful surprise. The food is expertly prepared and beautifully presented, reflecting the restaurant's commitment to quality. The attentive and welcoming staff ensure a pleasant dining experience, even for late-night diners. With its bustling atmosphere frequented by locals, Trattoria da Giulio is a testament to its reputation for delivering exceptional value and outstanding traditional fare. Located near Piazza Anfiteatro in the heart of Lucca, it offers a convenient and inviting setting to enjoy authentic Tuscan cuisine.

Via delle Conce 45 - Telephone +39 0583 55948

4. Buca di Sant'Antonio

Buca di Sant'Antonio is a culinary gem nestled between Piazza Anfiteatro and Piazza Napoleone, offering a classic dining experience within Lucca's medieval walls. Renowned as a city classic, this restaurant is a must-visit for those seeking to indulge. Their menu boasts excellent traditional Tuscan fare complemented by a wide selection of wines. The professional and attentive staff create a welcoming atmosphere from the moment you step inside, making you feel right at home. The restaurant's charming ambiance, adorned with typical Tuscan rural accents, sets the stage for a memorable dining experience. During warmer seasons, patrons can enjoy outdoor dining on the romantic patio just off the street. Buca di Sant'Antonio prides itself on serving classic Tuscan recipes made with the freshest ingredients, ensuring a delightful and inviting family dining experience. With its rich history dating back to the 19th century, Buca di Sant'Antonio offers exceptional value and authentic Tuscan cuisine in the heart of Lucca's historic center. Via della Cervia, 3 - Telephone: +39 0583 55881

5. Celide

Celide offers fresh and flavorful cuisine, with a particular emphasis on high-quality fish dishes. For an optimal dining experience, be sure to inquire about their daily menu, which changes regularly to showcase fresh and creatively prepared offerings. The restaurant's ambiance exudes a cool and elegant vibe, enhanced by its charming red-brick walls. Drawing crowds of locals, Celide maintains a reputation for serving food of exceptional quality at reasonable prices. The attentive and accommodating service ensures that every guest feels well taken care of, with staff readily available to translate the Italian menu upon request. Although situated just outside the bustling center of Lucca, Celide's location in front of the medieval walls adds to its allure, making it a hidden gem for those seeking delicious cuisine in a relaxed yet sophisticated setting.

Viale Giusti 25 - Telephone: +39 0583 469261

Wine Bars and Pubs

Vinarkia della Pavona: Vinarkia della Pavona offers a lively atmosphere with zingy cocktails and an extensive selection of Italian wines. The vintage-glam decor features heavily beamed ceilings, glossy dark-wood booths, and charming hanging baskets and barrels. Guests can enjoy affordable wines by the glass and receive personalized recommendations from the friendly owners, Nicola and Rebecca. Be sure to try their signature cocktails like the rum-based Marley Fizz or the refreshing Mamacita with watermelon and Campari.

Dal Bardo: Situated in the north of the old town, Dal Bardo is a hidden gem of a cocktail bar boasting a quaint and inviting ambiance. Adorned with faded vintage tiles and knobbly brick walls, the bar offers an array of curious liqueurs, tonics, and mixers. Guests can relax in the low-lit courtyard adorned with wine-colored parasols and indulge in classic Italian aperitivos like the Aperol Spritz served with delectable platters of bruschetta and ham.

De Cervesia: De Cervesia is a vibrant craft beer specialist known for its eclectic selection of ales, IPAs, and stouts from around the world. The tangerine walls are adorned with colorful banknotes, reflecting the diverse range of beers available. Brewing enthusiasts can chat with the youthful staff and enjoy pints of beer either inside the cozy establishment or outside on the curb. It's the perfect stop on a bar crawl for those seeking unique and flavorful brews.

Caffe Santa Zita: With its elegant art deco design, Caffe Santa Zita offers a glamorous setting for a relaxing afternoon or evening. The sage-colored bar trimmed with gold accents and vintage glass ice-cream bowls adds a touch of sophistication. Guests can enjoy aperitivi and snacks in this old-school tearoom, sampling dainty cakes and tarts from the counter. Drop by around 6pm for a taste of luxury and a glimpse into Lucca's vintage charm.

Franklin'33: Franklin'33 is a modern cocktail bar located in the heart of the walled old town, offering a theatrical experience reminiscent of the 1930s. Scarlet curtains, tattooed barmen, and vintage signage create an atmosphere of nostalgia. Guests can enjoy classic cocktails like the negroni or sazerac while basking in the cozy glow of chandeliers and pendant lamps.

Ciclo Divino: Located near the Piazza dell'Anfiteatro, Ciclo Divino is a hip wine bar known for its minimalist decor and affordable wine selection. Bicycles hang from metal racks, adding an artistic flair to the space. Guests can enjoy by-the-glass wines paired with tasty bruschetta served by friendly staff. Despite its small size, Ciclo Divino offers a taste of authentic after-work life in Lucca.

La Tana del Boia: La Tana del Boia is a renowned sandwich shop offering an informal yet inviting atmosphere for sharing nibbles and drinks. Guests can relax at small marble-topped tables facing the ancient, canopied entrance while enjoying top-quality food and drink. Fresh bread, charcuterie, cheese boards, and Italian beers are among the offerings, accompanied by mellow jazz music selected by owner Frederico.

Evening Entertainment

Nightclubs and Dancing

If you're looking to dance the night away in Lucca, you're in luck! Here are three popular nightclubs that cater to different tastes and preferences:

Seven Apples:

Renowned for its energetic atmosphere and themed parties, Seven Apples is a favorite among both locals and tourists. Whether you're into electronic music or live DJs, this nightclub promises a vibrant and lively experience that will keep you dancing until the early hours of the morning.

Divina Disco Club:

Located within the walls of an ancient church, Divina Disco Club offers a truly unique nightlife experience. With a diverse mix of music genres and a mesmerizing light show, this nightclub provides an immersive and unforgettable atmosphere for party-goers looking to dance and socialize.

Country Club:

Situated just outside Lucca's city walls, Country Club is a spacious nightclub known for its diverse music selection and lively crowd. Whether you're into hip-hop, pop, or electronic beats, this venue offers something for everyone and promises a memorable night out on the town.

Cultural Events and Shows

Lucca offers a rich cultural scene beyond its bars and nightclubs. Here are some venues and events that highlight the city's cultural diversity:

Teatro del Giglio: Step into the historic Teatro del Giglio to experience a wide array of performances, ranging from opera and ballet to concerts and theatrical productions. This iconic theater provides a platform for both local talent and international artists, making it a must-visit for culture enthusiasts.

Lucca Comics & Games: Calling all fans of comics, manga, and gaming! Lucca hosts an annual event known as Lucca Comics & Games, which is a paradise for enthusiasts of these genres. The event features exhibitions, workshops, cosplay contests, and more, drawing visitors from around the world to celebrate their passion for pop culture.

Museo della Cattedrale: Delve into the art and history of Lucca by visiting the Museum of the Cathedral, located near the breathtaking Lucca Cathedral. This museum offers insight into the city's religious and artistic heritage, showcasing treasures such as sculptures, paintings, and religious artifacts. It's a must-visit for anyone interested in exploring Lucca's cultural identity.

Food and Night Markets

Lucca's culinary scene is a vital part of its nightlife, offering a delightful array of flavors and experiences. Here are some places where you can immerse yourself in the city's gastronomic delights:

Antica Drogheria: Step into this historic shop to discover a treasure trove of local products and delicacies. From olive oils and balsamic vinegars to pasta, cheeses, and cured meats, Antica Drogheria offers a wide variety of gourmet delights. Food enthusiasts will delight in exploring the shelves and selecting items to take home as souvenirs of their visit to Lucca.

Antica Pasticceria Taddeucci: Indulge your sweet tooth at this charming bakery, which has been delighting customers with traditional pastries and cakes since 1881. From delicate pasticcini to rich chocolate tortes, Antica Pasticceria Taddeucci offers a tempting selection of treats that are sure to satisfy any craving.

San Francesco Night Market: Experience the bustling atmosphere of Lucca's San Francesco Night Market, held every Thursday evening. Here, you'll find a vibrant array of local products, including fresh produce, cheeses, meats, and artisan crafts. Take your time exploring the stalls, sampling the offerings, and soaking up the lively ambiance of this beloved market.

SHOPPING IN LUCCA

- Markets and Bazaars
- Artisanal Crafts and Souvenirs
- Fashion Boutiques and Designer Stores

SHOPPING IN LUCCA

Markets and Bazaars

Lucca's marketplaces, particularly the antiques market, are excellent places to look for hidden treasures. There is a good chance that there will be a market when you visit the city, as several are held each month.

Antiques Market

The antiques market takes place on the third Saturday and Sunday of the month. It is mostly concentrated around Piazza San Giusto and Piazza Antelminelli, but it extends across many of the town's streets and squares. It attracts approximately 220 exhibitors from all across Italy and is regarded as one of the country's most important.

Handicrafts Market

This is a market where you may buy things made by local craftspeople. The market takes place primarily at Piazza S. Giusto on the last Sunday of each month.

Lucca Weekly Market

The regular market is held every Wednesday and Saturday at the Le Tagliate parking lot. Clothing, linen, household items, and food are the most common items available.

Farmers' Market

The farmers' market is held every Saturday (and Wednesday in the summer) in Foro Boario. There are roughly twenty local agricultural producers selling a variety of food products, including fresh from nearby Versilia and a florist's stand. This is the ideal spot to find traditional and seasonal items.

MercoledìBio

MercoledìBio, an organic and fair-trade food market held on Wednesday afternoons in Piazza San Francesco, brings together local producers.

Artisanal Crafts and Souvenirs

Lucca's charm extends far beyond its historic walls and captivating piazzas. Nestled within its streets are a treasure trove of artisanal workshops and shops brimming with unique souvenirs, handcrafted keepsakes, and local delights. Whether you seek a piece of Lucca to bring home or a gift imbued with Italian artistry, here's a guide to help you navigate Lucca's artisanal scene:

A Touch of Tuscany:

Ceramica Benadelli: Stepping into Ceramica Benadelli is like stepping back in time. This historic workshop, established in 1860, carries on the Lucca tradition of exquisite ceramics. Imagine browsing shelves adorned with hand-painted plates, vases, and decorative objects, each one a testament to generations-old craftsmanship. These beautiful pieces, often featuring Tuscan landscapes or floral motifs, are the perfect way to bring a touch of Lucca's artistic heritage home with you.

Manifatture Toscane: Embrace the essence of Tuscany with handcrafted leather goods from Manifatture Toscane. This local workshop specializes in beautiful leather bags, wallets, and accessories, all meticulously crafted using traditional techniques. The rich aroma of leather fills the air as you explore their collection, each piece a unique blend of functionality and timeless style. A bag or wallet from Manifatture Toscane is a souvenir that will stand the test of time.

A Foodie's Paradise:

Vecchi Sapori di Lucca:Indulge your taste buds at Vecchi Sapori di Lucca, a haven for local delicacies and gourmet food products. Step inside and be greeted by the enticing aroma of cured meats, cheeses, and freshly baked treats. Their shelves are overflowing with local specialties like farro (an ancient grain), top-quality olive oil, and bottles of Lucca's signature condiment, "garfagnana green pesto." Don't forget to sample their selection of local wines and liquors – perfect for recreating a taste of Lucca back home.

Zaza Bakery: For those with a sweet tooth, Zaza Bakery is a must-visit. This charming bakery entices passersby with the aroma of freshly baked bread, pastries, and Lucca's signature cake, "buccellato." Imagine rows of golden-brown cookies, delicate pastries, and slices of fluffy buccellato, a ring-shaped cake studded with candied fruit and nuts. A box of treats from Zaza Bakery is a delicious way to share a taste of Lucca with friends and family.

Unique Souvenirs:

La Tela di Penelope: For a truly unique souvenir, head to La Tela di Penelope, a workshop dedicated to the traditional art of Lunigiana lace. Here, skilled artisans meticulously create intricate lace patterns using time-honored techniques. From delicate handkerchiefs to ornate tablecloths, each piece is a masterpiece of patience and artistry. Watching the artisans work and learning about the history of Lunigiana lace is an experience in itself.

Bottega Guimarello: Immerse yourself in the world of papermaking at Bottega Guimarello. This historic workshop, established in 1344, is one of the oldest continuously operating paper mills in Europe. Witness the fascinating process of transforming raw materials into beautiful sheets of handmade paper. The shop offers a variety of paper products, from blank notebooks to decorative stationery, all made with the same techniques used for centuries. A unique souvenir with a rich history.

Beyond the Shops:

Weekly Farmer's Market: Explore the vibrant weekly farmer's market in Piazza dell'Anfiteatro. Here, you'll find an abundance of fresh local produce, handmade crafts, and regional specialties. It's the perfect place to soak up the local atmosphere and find unique treasures.

Tips for Souvenir Shopping

Support Local Artisans: Look for shops displaying the "Made in Italy" label to ensure you're supporting local artisans and traditional crafts.

Haggling: While not as common in Italy as in other parts of the world, friendly negotiation, particularly at street markets, can sometimes yield a slightly better price.

Bring a Reusable Bag: Lucca is increasingly eco-conscious, so consider bringing a reusable bag to avoid single-use plastic bags.

With its rich history and vibrant artistic scene, Lucca offers a treasure trove of artisanal delights waiting to be discovered. So, take your time, explore the shops, and bring home a piece of Lucca's

Fashion Boutiques and Designer Stores

Lucca may be a charming walled city steeped in history, but don't underestimate its fashionable offerings! While it might not rival the fashion capitals of Milan or Florence, Lucca boasts a delightful selection of boutiques and designer stores catering to a variety of styles and budgets. Whether you crave timeless Italian elegance or a touch of contemporary flair, Lucca's fashion scene promises a treasure trove waiting to be discovered.

For the Discerning Fashionista

De Simoni: Established in 1885, this family-run haven offers a curated selection of menswear and womenswear from established Italian and international fashion houses, alongside their own ready-to-wear line. Imagine browsing sleek Max Mara coats next to a stunning piece from a rising Italian designer, all under one roof. De Simoni also boasts a range of shoes, bags, and accessories, and their expert tailoring services ensure a perfect fit for any garment.

Vanitas: This boutique is a treasure trove of high-end designer clothing, shoes, and accessories for women.

Think Valentino gowns brushing shoulders with the latest Dolce & Gabbana collections, alongside pieces from emerging Italian talents. Be prepared to be dazzled by the sheer variety and exclusivity offered at Vanitas.

Modern Boutiques with Italian Flair

Dixie: A local favorite, Dixie offers a carefully curated selection of contemporary womenswear from popular Italian and international brands like Max Mara, Brunello Cucinelli, and Pinko. Picture a bright and inviting space filled with on-trend pieces that are perfect for a night out or a day of exploring the city's historical gems.

Manila Boutique: Catering to a younger, fashion-forward clientele, Manila Boutique offers a trendy selection of women's clothing, shoes, and accessories. Here, you'll find a focus on emerging Italian designers and independent labels, ensuring you discover unique pieces that will make you stand out. Don't miss their small selection of vintage clothing, adding a touch of eclectic charm to your shopping spree.

Beyond Clothing

Il Panda: A family-run shop since 1936, Il Panda is a haven for those seeking high-quality shoes and leather goods. Picture yourself browsing shelves overflowing with Italian-made boots, shoes, bags, and leather accessories from top brands. They also have a great selection of hosiery and tights, ensuring every detail of your outfit is perfectly polished.

Wolford Boutique: Specializing in luxury hosiery, lingerie, and shapewear, Wolford Boutique caters to a variety of styles and sizes. From their renowned tights and stockings to bodysuits and shapewear, their collection promises to flatter every body type.

OUTDOOR ACTIVITIES

- Cycling and Walking Tours
- Hiking and Nature Trails
- River Activities and Boat Tours

OUTDOOR ACTIVITIES

Cycling and Walking Tours

Bicycling is a common and long-established mode of transportation for residents of Lucca and the surrounding Tuscan region. Nearly everyone possesses a bicycle for commuting inside the city or to neighboring regions.

Even if you're not a seasoned cyclist, embarking on a bike tour is an excellent way to discover the area, especially since Lucca is incredibly bike-friendly.

Begin Your Adventure on Lucca's Walls

When seeking advice on where to start your tour in Lucca, locals will invariably suggest the Walls. Covering a distance of just 4.22 km, this route offers a unique vantage point to admire the city from above. It's particularly enjoyable for families with children. On weekends, you'll encounter numerous residents doing the same, regardless of how many times they've ridden the path before.

The cycling track forms a complete loop, and there are multiple access points for reaching all the major tourist attractions.

The Serchio River, one of Tuscany's primary waterways, meanders through Lucca, just a short distance from the city's ancient walls. Spanning 22 kilometers, the Serchio River Park offers opportunities for exploration on foot or by bicycle, traversing through the surrounding agricultural landscape, seamlessly integrated into its surroundings.

Two distinct routes await adventurers: the first forms a loop along both banks of the river, covering approximately 11 kilometers from Ponte San Quirico to Ponte San Pietro. Along the way, you'll encounter the Ponte della Musica Popolare, with a quaint beach nestled below, providing a refreshing respite from the summer heat. The second route extends from Ponte San Quirico to Ponte a Moriano, spanning 7 kilometers, albeit without the loop feature.

Explore Lucca's surrounding areas on longer and leisurely bike rides, discovering the stunning Marina di

Vecchiano, Versilia Coast, and Pisa. These routes may be a bit lengthier, but they offer a smooth and flat terrain, making them accessible for riders of all levels. Here are our top picks:

Ponte a Moriano to Bocca di Serchio

Follow the serene path of the Serchio River Park as it winds its way toward the sea. Beginning at Ponte a Moriano, pedal along the riverbanks towards Bocca di Serchio, covering approximately 35 kilometers. Traverse through the idyllic fields of Migliarino, with this route paying homage to Giacomo Puccini, as it passes through his birthplace of Lucca and Lago Massaciuccoli.

Upon reaching Bocca di Serchio, situated in Marina di Vecchiano, you have further options to explore. Turn right along the shoreline to reach Viareggio in Versilia. This stretch of the Versilia coast, from Marina di Vecchiano to Viareggio via Torre del Lago Puccini, boasts a pristine free beach. For those interested, a map of the route is readily available.

Alternatively, veer left to discover the enchanting San Rossore Park, from where you can conveniently journey to Pisa. The direct route from Bocca di Serchio to Pisa city is a mere 15 kilometers.

Ciclovia Versilia (Versilia cycle route)

For a delightful day in Versilia, embark on the scenic and straightforward Ciclovia della Versilia, tracing the coastline from Viareggio to Marina di Massa. Stretching over 28 kilometers, it stands as Italy's most coastal cycle path, accessible to all riders. Along the way, indulge in picturesque stops for an aperitivo at sunset, with the mesmerizing sea as your backdrop.

For experienced cyclists seeking exhilarating adventures, Lucca and its surrounding regions offer boundless opportunities to explore. Venture into the Apuan Alps and Garfagnana area, where rare beauty awaits with a plethora of roads and trails to conquer. From vantage points like Passo del Vestito and Passo del Cipollaio, marvel at panoramic views of marble caves juxtaposed against the azure sea below.

Discover the enchanting allure of Isola Santa, an ancient medieval village partially submerged in a tranquil lake, offering a hauntingly picturesque setting.

Alternatively, trace the historic paths of the Via Francigena, the famed Pilgrim Road stretching 1800 kilometers from Canterbury to Rome, which intersects through Lucca. Here, a myriad of captivating routes awaits your exploration.

Looking to rent a bike in Lucca? Numerous options abound within the city walls. Cicli Bizzarri and Biciclette Poli, both located in Piazza Santa Maria, offer well-equipped rental services. However, for a tailored experience inclusive of drop-off services and personalized tours, Tuscany Ride a Bike stands out as the ideal choice.

In Lucca, cyclists of all levels can revel in a diverse array of riding experiences. Whether you yearn for coastal vistas, mountainous terrain, or leisurely city wall strolls, the city and its surroundings cater to your cycling desires. And for those craving an off-road adventure, numerous mountain biking trails await exploration, promising thrills amidst breathtaking landscapes.

Hiking and Nature Trails

1. Historical Walls of Lucca

Elevation Gain: 51 meters

Route Type: Loop

Distance: 4.3 kilometers

Duration: Approximately 56 minutes

Difficulty: Easy

Embark on this delightful 4.3-kilometer loop trail near Lucca, Tuscany, and immerse yourself in the beauty of its historic walls. Considered an easy route, this trail offers a leisurely stroll or a brisk walk, taking you through captivating scenery and rich history. Whether you're a mountain biker, road biker, or runner, this trail caters to all, promising a memorable experience.

Highlights of the Trail:

Scenic Beauty: This trail winds along the historic walls of Lucca, offering panoramic views of the cityscape and surrounding landscape. Immerse yourself in the serene atmosphere as you traverse the paved road, lined with lush greenery and picturesque vistas.

Historic Landmarks: Along the route, you'll encounter various historic landmarks and points of interest. Take the opportunity to explore the fascinating history of Lucca as you pass by ancient ramparts, majestic gates, and charming gardens.

Opportunities for Exploration: The trail provides ample opportunities to pause and explore the historic city center. Wander through narrow cobblestone streets, discover hidden piazzas, and admire architectural marvels as you venture off the beaten path.

Relaxation and Refreshment: Need a break? There are plenty of benches and shaded spots along the trail where you can rest and rejuvenate. Take in the tranquil ambiance, enjoy a picnic, or simply bask in the beauty of your surroundings.

Dog-Friendly: Bring your furry friend along for the adventure!This trail is dog-friendly, however dogs need to be leashed. Let your canine companion explore alongside you as you uncover the wonders of Lucca.

Trailhead: The route begins at Baluardo Santa Maria, conveniently located near the Antico Caffè delle Mura. Kick-start your journey with a refreshing beverage or a quick bite before setting off on your exploration of Lucca's historic walls.

Best Times to Visit: Plan your adventure between April and September to make the most of favorable weather conditions and pleasant temperatures. Whether you're seeking a leisurely stroll or an invigorating workout, this trail promises an unforgettable experience for all.

So, lace up your shoes, grab your camera, and embark on a journey through time and beauty along Lucca's historic walls trail. With its scenic vistas, rich history, and leisurely pace, this trail invites you to discover the enchanting allure of one of Tuscany's most cherished destinations.

Frequently Asked Questions About Hiking Trails in Lucca:

What varieties of hiking trails can be found in Lucca?

Lucca offers a variety of hiking trails catering to different interests and skill levels. On AllTrails.com, you'll find 16 hiking trails, 9 mountain biking trails, 7 running trails, and more, providing options for hikers, bikers, and runners alike.

Among the Lucca footpaths, which one ascends the highest?

The Aqueduct Road: Lucca - Pisa trail boasts the most elevation gain in Lucca, with an ascent of 854 meters. This challenging trail rewards hikers with stunning views and a sense of accomplishment. The Lucca - Montecarlo - Marlia trail follows closely behind with 784 meters of elevation gain.

Which is Lucca's most well-liked and challenging trail?

The most popular and challenging trail in Lucca is The Aqueduct Road: Lucca - Pisa. With a 4.3-star rating from 37 reviews, this trail offers a rigorous workout and breathtaking scenery, making it a favorite among experienced hikers seeking a thrilling adventure.

Are there running trails available in Lucca?

Yes, Lucca offers a variety of running trails for fitness enthusiasts. According to AllTrails.com, there are 7 running trails in Lucca. The most popular among them is The Historical Walls of Lucca, which has an average rating of 4.6 stars from 115 community reviews. Lace up your shoes and hit the trails for an invigorating run amidst stunning scenery.

Are there biking trails available in Lucca?

Absolutely! Lucca boasts 14 biking trails, offering cyclists the opportunity to explore the region's diverse landscapes and attractions. The Historical Walls of Lucca is the most popular biking trail, with an average rating of 4.6 stars from 115 community reviews. Whether you're a beginner or a seasoned cyclist, Lucca's biking trails cater to all skill levels and interests. So, hop on your bike and embark on an unforgettable ride through picturesque scenery and charming villages.

River Activities and Boat Tours

1. Cinque Terre Tour Small Group Tour from Lucca

Embark on a captivating journey from Lucca to the enchanting seaside villages of Cinque Terre, renowned for their vibrant colors and breathtaking coastal landscapes. Travel in a small group and experience the beauty of this UNESCO-listed destination with personalized attention and service.

As you journey along the spectacular Ligurian coastline, marvel at the dramatic contours of the rugged cliffs and azure waters. Whether by train or boat, soak in the scenic beauty that surrounds you, immersing yourself in the charm of terraced fishing towns that cascade down the rocky hillside to meet the sparkling sea.

Explore picturesque villages such as Riomaggiore, Vernazza, and Manarola, each offering its own unique allure and photogenic beauty. Wander through narrow alleyways, admire colorful houses clinging to the cliffs, and soak up the laid-back atmosphere of coastal life.

Throughout the tour, your knowledgeable guide will provide insights into the history, culture, and traditions of Cinque Terre, offering a deeper understanding of this captivating destination. With a small group size, you'll enjoy a more personalized experience, ensuring ample opportunities to ask questions and interact with your guide.

Discover why Cinque Terre has captivated travelers and photographers alike, and create unforgettable memories amidst the stunning scenery of the Italian Riviera.

Enjoy a hassle-free and immersive experience with our inclusive tour package. Here's what's included:

Driver: Sit back, relax, and let our experienced driver navigate the scenic routes, ensuring a comfortable journey throughout the day.

Tour Leader: Benefit from the expertise of our knowledgeable tour leader, who will accompany you throughout the day, providing insights into the destinations, history, and culture of Cinque Terre.

Transport: Travel in style and comfort with air-conditioned transportation provided by a minivan or minibus, ensuring a smooth and enjoyable ride between Lucca and Cinque Terre.

Tickets: Gain access to transportation options, including ferryboat and train tickets (weather permitting), allowing you to explore the coastal villages of Cinque Terre with ease.

Gratuities: Leave the tipping to us. Gratuities for drivers, guides, and other service staff are included in the tour package, ensuring a hassle-free experience.

Lunch: Indulge in a delicious lunch included in the tour, allowing you to savor authentic Italian cuisine at a local restaurant or trattoria.

Meeting and Pickup Details:

Meeting Point: Porta San Pietro, Sortita Porta S. Pietro, 55100 Lucca LU, Italy

End Point: The activity concludes back at the meeting point, ensuring convenient drop-off after a day of exploration.

KID-FRIENDLY ATTRACTIONS IN LUCCA

- Family-Friendly Accommodation Options
- Tips for Traveling with Children
- Educational and Interactive Activities for Kids

KID-FRIENDLY ATTRACTIONS IN LUCCA

Family-Friendly Accommodation Options

1. Albergo San Martino

Address: Via Della Dogana 9

Price: 156$

Conveniently located in Lucca's Centro Storico district, the cozy Albergo San Martino sits near the Roman Catholic St Martin Cathedral. With the iconic Guinigi Medieval Tower just steps away, this hotel boasts 28 comfortable rooms and a welcoming lounge bar.

You'll find yourself within easy reach of Lucca's historic treasures, with the medieval plaza of Piazza dell'Anfiteatro just 0.8 km away and the charming Via Fillungo at 0.9 km. The vibrant city center is a mere 1 km stroll from the hotel, offering access to Lucca's renowned attractions.

For those keen to explore further afield, the Porta Elisa City Wall is just a short ride away. Whether you're here for sightseeing or relaxation, Albergo San Martino offers a convenient and comfortable base for your stay in Lucca.

2. Resort Dei Limoni

Address: Via Nuova Per Pisa 1952

Price: 157$

Nestled in the picturesque surroundings of Lucca, the 5-star Resort Dei Limoni offers a luxurious retreat. Conveniently located just 4.4 km from Lucca State Library and 1.5 km from the International Academy of Italian Cuisine, our resort promises an exceptional stay.

Our dedicated team of multilingual staff is at your service, ensuring a seamless experience from the moment you arrive. Whether you require airport transfer, assistance at our 24-hour front desk, or complimentary shuttle service, we are here to cater to your every need.

While the bustling city center is just 5 km away, allowing easy access to Lucca's vibrant attractions, our tranquil resort offers a peaceful escape from the urban hustle and bustle. Additionally, the scenic Bagno Gioia is only a few minutes away by car, perfect for a leisurely day by the water.

Free Wi-Fi in rooms	Outdoor swimming pool
Luggage storage	Flat-screen TV
Poolside snack bar	Lift
Snack bar	In-room breakfast
Paid airport shuttle	Sun loungers

3. La Boheme Bed & Breakfast

Address: Via Del Moro, 2

Price: 147$

Located in the heart of Lucca, the 2-star La Boheme Bed & Breakfast offers guests a cozy retreat within walking distance of Domus Romana. Our charming venue provides complimentary WiFi throughout the hotel, ensuring you stay connected during your visit.

Just 950 meters from Porta Elisa City Wall and 0.9 km from the Roman Catholic St Martin Cathedral, our property boasts a central location that allows easy exploration of Lucca's historic landmarks. Additionally, Lucca City Hall is situated nearby, offering guests convenient access to the city's administrative center.

While staying at La Boheme Bed & Breakfast, guests can enjoy easy access to Via Fillungo and other nearby attractions, making it an ideal choice for travelers seeking to experience the best of Lucca.

Wi-Fi	Back massage
Luggage storage	Head massage
Welcome drink	Full body massage
Coffee shop	Foot massage
Paid airport shuttle	Laundry

4. Lucca In Villa Lucrezia

Address: Viale Luigi Cadorna 30

Price: 116$

Nestled in the charming Lucca Historical Center district, the 2-star Lucca In Villa Lucrezia offers elegant accommodation just a short stroll from the iconic Guinigi Medieval Tower, located approximately 750 meters away. Guests will find themselves within easy reach of Le mura di Lucca, allowing for convenient exploration of the city's historic walls.

Situated 1 km from Lucca city center and 25 km from Galileo Galilei airport, our property offers a tranquil retreat in the heart of the city. Domus Romana is located 1.5 km away, while City Wall is just a short ride from the hotel, allowing guests to easily discover Lucca's many attractions.

At Lucca In Villa Lucrezia, guests can enjoy comfortable accommodation and convenient access to the city's landmarks, making it an ideal choice for travelers seeking a memorable stay in Lucca.

5. Hotel Carignano

Address: Via Per Sant'Alessio, 3680 Localita Carignano

Price: 79$

Located just a 10-minute drive from Serchio, Hotel Carignano Lucca offers guests a range of amenities including free parking, an outdoor swimming pool, and a sun terrace. Situated approximately 5 km from the center of Lucca, the hotel provides easy access to the city's attractions, with the iconic Guinigi Medieval Tower just 4.4 km away.

For travelers arriving by air, the hotel boasts a convenient location, with Galileo Galilei airport reachable in just a 34-minute drive. Additionally, guests can explore the historic walls of Lucca, known as Le mura di Lucca, which are only a short drive from the hotel.

Whether you're seeking relaxation by the poolside or eager to explore the sights of Lucca, Hotel Carignano offers a convenient base for your stay in this picturesque Tuscan city.

6. Hotel Villa Cheli

Address: Via Nuova Per Pisa 1798

Price: 100$

Nestled in the heart of Lucca, Hotel Villa Cheli offers a delightful retreat with its range of amenities, including complimentary self-parking, an inviting outdoor swimming pool, and a sun-drenched terrace. Just a brief 10-minute drive from Porta San Pietro, the hotel provides convenient access to the city's attractions, with the iconic Guinigi Medieval Tower situated less than 4.3 km away.

While centrally located, the property provides easy access to explore the charming streets and historical landmarks of Lucca. Guests can venture to the nearby Roman San Michele in Foro Catholic Church, a cultural gem awaiting exploration just a short drive away.

Whether seeking relaxation by the poolside or eager to explore the rich history and culture of Lucca, Hotel Villa Cheli offers a welcoming retreat for guests to immerse themselves in the beauty of this enchanting Tuscan city.

7. Albergo Celide

Address: Viale Giuseppe Giusti 25

Price: 143$

Conveniently situated in the charming Lucca Historical Center district, Albergo Celide offers a comfortable retreat within easy reach of the iconic St Martin Cathedral. Guests can enjoy the added luxury of a hot tub and Turkish bath, perfect for unwinding after a day of exploration, along with the convenience of a 24-hour bar steps away from a nearby train station.

With the city center just 1 km away, the accommodation provides easy access to Lucca's main attractions. Guests can stroll to the historic Porta Elisa City Wall or explore the bustling Via Fillungo, both within a short walk from the hotel. For those seeking a taste of Tuscan elegance, the renowned Elegant Tuscan Window-Shop is just a 22-minute walk away.

With its central location and array of amenities, including a hot tub, Turkish bath, and 24-hour bar, Albergo Celide offers guests a comfortable and convenient stay in the heart of Lucca.

Tips for Traveling with Children

Lucca, with its charming car-free center, rich history, and delicious food, is a perfect destination for a family vacation. However, planning a trip with children requires extra consideration. Here's a comprehensive guide packed with tips to ensure your Lucca adventure is filled with fun and happy memories for everyone:

Planning Your Trip:

Accommodation: Opt for family-friendly hotels or apartments with amenities like cribs, high chairs, and swimming pools. Consider staying near a piazza or park to give your little ones space to run around.

Travel Time: If traveling long distances, break up the journey with rest stops or plan activities to keep your children entertained.

Light Packing: Pack versatile clothing for changeable weather and comfortable walking shoes for exploring the city walls. Don't forget essentials like sunscreen, hats, and wet wipes.

Keeping the Little Ones Entertained:

Exploring the Walls: Lucca's car-free walls are a haven for families. Rent bikes (including children's bikes and trailers) and enjoy a leisurely ride with stunning views of the city. Playgrounds scattered along the walls provide great pit stops for energetic little ones.

Imagine the delight on your children's faces as they breeze along Lucca's ancient walls, taking in the panoramic cityscape. Rent children's bikes and trailers for a safe and enjoyable experience for the whole family. Playgrounds strategically placed along the walls offer welcome breaks for energetic little ones to release their pent-up energy.

Puppet Show: Head to Piazza Anfimiteatro for a delightful puppet show. The traditional marionette shows are a fun and captivating way to introduce children to Italian culture.

Step into the world of wonder at Piazza Anfimiteatro. Here, talented puppeteers bring classic stories to life with colorful marionette shows. Your children will be mesmerized by the intricate movements and dramatic narratives, sparking their imaginations and introducing them to a unique form of Italian theater.

Interactive Museums: Lucca offers museums that cater to young minds. The Palazzo Guinigi with its quirky hanging garden is a unique experience, while the Museum of Comics and Illustrations boasts interactive exhibits that will spark children's imaginations.

For a touch of whimsy, head to the Palazzo Guinigi. This medieval tower boasts a surprising secret – a hanging garden at the top! Take the winding staircase (not recommended for those with small children or stroller users) and be rewarded with breathtaking views and a truly unique experience. If your children are fans of comics and cartoons, the Museum of Comics and Illustrations is a must-visit. Interactive exhibits and displays featuring popular characters will keep them entertained for hours.

Gelato Time: No Italian adventure is complete without gelato! Lucca boasts numerous gelato shops offering delicious flavors. Make a stop for a refreshing treat and enjoy watching your kids' faces light up.

As the Italian saying goes, "Don't cry over spilled gelato!" Lucca's numerous gelato shops offer a delightful dilemma – choosing from a vast array of flavors. After a day of exploring, indulge in a refreshing scoop (or two) of gelato. The happy smiles on your children's faces will be priceless.

A Culinary Adventure:

Kid-Friendly Restaurants: Many restaurants in Lucca offer children's menus with familiar options like pasta dishes and pizzas. Look for places with outdoor seating, perfect for keeping an eye on little ones.

Finding restaurants that cater to even the pickiest eaters is a breeze in Lucca. Many restaurants offer children's menus featuring familiar favorites like pasta with simple tomato sauce or cheese pizzas. Opt for places with outdoor seating, allowing your children some space to wiggle while you enjoy your meal.

Picnics in the Park: Pack a picnic lunch and head to one of Lucca's beautiful parks like Giardino Botanico or Parco della Mura. Enjoy a relaxing afternoon amidst nature, letting the kids run free.

Lucca's parks are oases of green amidst the historical city center. Pack a picnic basket filled with fresh bread, cheese, cured meats, and seasonal fruits for a delightful lunch break in the park. The Giardino Botanico (Botanical Garden) offers a beautiful setting with a variety of plants and flowers to explore. Parco della Mura, located along the city walls, provides ample space for children to run around and burn off energy.

Cooking Class: Bond with your children over a fun cooking class. Many cooking schools offer family-friendly classes where you can learn to make traditional Tuscan dishes together. It's a rewarding experience and a great way to introduce children to new flavors.

For a unique and memorable experience, sign up for a family cooking class. Many cooking schools in Lucca offer courses designed specifically for families

Educational and Interactive Activities for Kids

Lucca isn't just a charming walled city steeped in history; it's also a playground for curious minds. Beyond the delicious gelato and captivating piazzas, Lucca offers a wealth of educational and interactive activities that will spark your children's imaginations and turn sightseeing into an unforgettable learning experience. Here's a guide packed with ideas to keep your little explorers engaged throughout your Lucca adventure:

Step Back in Time:

Lucca City Walls: Transform yourselves into time travelers! Lucca's car-free walls, dating back to the Renaissance era, offer a unique opportunity to walk through history. Rent bikes (including children's options) and embark on a family adventure along the ramparts. Imagine yourselves as medieval knights defending the city, all while enjoying panoramic views. Interactive panels along the walls provide fascinating historical tidbits, making the experience both educational and engaging.

Guidi Tower Climb: Challenge yourselves to a climb up the Torre Guinigi, a medieval tower renowned for its quirky hanging garden. As you ascend the narrow staircase (not recommended for very young children or strollers), imagine knights using the tower for lookout purposes. Reaching the top is rewarded with breathtaking city views and a chance to explore the unique hanging garden – a true conversation starter!

Roman Amphitheatre Exploration: Head to Piazza dell'Anfiteatro, a bustling piazza built upon the remains of a Roman amphitheatre. Imagine gladiatorial contests taking place centuries ago! While the amphitheatre itself isn't accessible for exploration, children can use their imaginations to recreate scenes from history while enjoying the lively atmosphere of the piazza.

Interactive Museums:

Museum of Comics and Illustrations: Calling all comic book fans! The Museum of Comics and Illustrations is a haven for creative minds. Interactive exhibits showcase the history of comics and illustrations, featuring popular Italian and international characters. Children can participate in workshops, drawing activities, and even create their own comic strips!

Lucca's Walls Museum: Delve deeper into the history of Lucca's impressive walls at the Lucca's Walls Museum. Interactive displays, models, and multimedia presentations bring the city's fortifications to life. Children can learn about different architectural styles, defensive strategies, and the daily lives of people who lived within the walls centuries ago.

Palazzo Mansi National Museum: Step into a world of Renaissance splendor at the Palazzo Mansi National Museum. While the opulent halls and stunning artwork might seem overwhelming for very young children, older kids can participate in scavenger hunts or family tours designed to spark their interest in art history and the lives of the wealthy families who resided in the palace.

Hands-on Learning:

Cooking Class Adventure: Bond with your children over a fun cooking class! Many cooking schools in Lucca offer family-friendly courses where you can learn to make traditional Tuscan dishes together. Roll out fresh pasta dough, create delicious pizza toppings, and enjoy the satisfaction of creating a meal together. This activity not only teaches children about different ingredients and cooking techniques but also creates lasting memories.

Medieval Workshop: Immerse yourselves in the world of medieval crafts at a local workshop. Many artisans offer workshops where children can learn the traditional techniques of leatherworking, pottery making, or paper marbling. Creating their own handcrafted souvenir is a rewarding experience that allows children to connect with the local culture and appreciate the skill of artisans.

Treasure Hunt in the Markets: Turn Lucca's vibrant markets into a learning adventure! Plan a treasure hunt, giving your children a list of items to find, like fresh local produce, traditional crafts, or specific types of flowers. This activity encourages exploration, teaches them about different products, and exposes them to the sights, sounds, and smells of the marketplace.

Beyond the Walls:

Day Trip to a Working Farm: Escape the city for a day trip to a working farm near Lucca. Many farms offer educational tours where children can learn about different farm animals, see crops being grown, and even participate in simple farm chores. This is a great opportunity for children to connect with nature and understand the origins of the food they eat.

Boat Ride on the Serchio River: Embark on a relaxing boat ride on the Serchio River, offering a different perspective of Lucca's beauty. Many companies offer family-friendly tours with commentary, pointing out historical landmarks and interesting flora and fauna along the riverbanks. This is a peaceful way to learn about Lucca's geography and environment while enjoying a scenic journey.

With a little creativity and these engaging activities, your trip to Lucca will be an educational adventure for the whole family. So, pack your sense of discovery and get ready to create lasting memories in this charming Italian city!

DAY TRIPS FROM LUCCA

- Pisa
- Florence
- Cinque Terre

DAY TRIPS FROM LUCCA

Pisa

While Pisa's Leaning Tower is its most iconic landmark, the city offers a wealth of attractions beyond this architectural marvel. Explore the charming medieval town, where Romanesque monuments and historic buildings abound. Here's what else Pisa has to offer:

Romanesque Monuments: Surrounding the Leaning Tower is a complex of stunning Romanesque structures, including the impressive 11th-century cathedral. Marvel at the intricate architecture and rich history of these ancient landmarks.

Scenic Riverfront: A picturesque river runs through Pisa, offering scenic views and tranquil spots for a leisurely stroll. Admire the medieval buildings lining the riverbanks and soak up the city's serene ambiance.

Cultural Gems: Pisa boasts an array of museums showcasing art, history, and science. Explore fascinating exhibits, from ancient artifacts to modern masterpieces, and delve into the city's rich cultural heritage.

Botanical Garden: Escape the hustle and bustle of the city and immerse yourself in nature at Pisa's botanical garden. Discover a diverse collection of plant species from around the world and enjoy a peaceful retreat amidst lush greenery.

Dining Delights: Indulge in the culinary delights of Pisa at its charming cafes, trattorias, and restaurants. Sample authentic Tuscan cuisine, from hearty pasta dishes to mouthwatering seafood specialties, and savor the flavors of Italy.

Shopping Extravaganza: Explore Pisa's vibrant streets lined with shops and boutiques, offering everything from locally crafted souvenirs to designer fashion. Browse for unique gifts, stylish clothing, and artisanal treasures to commemorate your visit.

Plan Ahead: If visiting during peak season, it's advisable to purchase tickets to the Leaning Tower in advance to avoid long queues and ensure entry to this iconic landmark.

Getting There: Traveling to Pisa by train is convenient, with frequent services departing from major cities like Florence. Opt for the San Rossore station for easy access to the Leaning Tower and Piazza dei Miracoli, located before Pisa Centrale, the city's main train station.

By immersing yourself in Pisa's rich history, culture, and natural beauty, you'll discover a city brimming with surprises and unforgettable experiences beyond its famous leaning landmark.

Florence

While a single day might not be enough to fully immerse yourself in all of Florence's treasures, you can still experience the essence of this magnificent city by focusing on its iconic landmarks and cultural highlights. Here's how to make the most of your day trip to Florence:

Piazza del Duomo: Begin your journey at the heart of Florence's historic center, the Piazza del Duomo. Marvel at the breathtaking Cathedral of Santa Maria del Fiore, with its distinctive dome, elegant bell tower, and mesmerizing facade. Don't miss the opportunity to climb to the top of the dome for panoramic views of the city.

Accademia Gallery: Delve into Renaissance art and sculpture at the Accademia Gallery, home to Michelangelo's masterpiece, the David statue. Admire this iconic sculpture up close and explore the gallery's impressive collection of Renaissance artworks.

Hidden Gems: Join a small group walking tour of Florence, led by knowledgeable guides who will unveil the city's hidden gems and lesser-known attractions. Discover charming alleyways, picturesque squares, and secret spots off the beaten path, gaining insight into Florence's rich history and culture along the way.

Discount Offer: Take advantage of a special offer on the Florence Walking Tour with David, which includes exclusive access to hidden gems and a visit to the Accademia to see the David statue. Use promo code ITALYMARTHA to enjoy a 5% discount on this enriching tour experience.

Train Travel: Traveling to Florence from Lucca is convenient and efficient, with frequent train services connecting the two cities. Catch a train from Lucca to Florence's main station, Santa Maria Novella, which departs multiple times per hour and takes approximately 1.25 to 1.75 hours. Along the way, you'll pass by charming towns like Montecatini Terme, Prato, and Pistoia, each offering its own unique attractions and allure.

By embarking on a day trip to Florence, you'll have the opportunity to soak up the city's vibrant atmosphere, admire its architectural wonders, and uncover its artistic treasures, leaving you with lasting memories of this cultural mecca in the heart of Tuscany.

Cinque Terre

Cinque Terre, meaning "Five Lands," isn't just a collection of picturesque villages clinging to cliffs; it's a UNESCO World Heritage Site bursting with vibrant colors, dramatic landscapes, and captivating beauty. And the best part? This coastal paradise is within reach for a captivating day trip from Lucca. Here's a comprehensive guide to plan your unforgettable Cinque Terre adventure:

Planning Your Journey:

Distance and Travel Time: Lucca and Cinque Terre are roughly 70 kilometers (43 miles) apart. The train journey is the most convenient and scenic option, taking approximately 1.5 hours. Alternatively, guided tours often include transportation by car or minivan, offering a more comfortable experience.

Choosing Your Mode of Transport:

Train: For a budget-friendly option, opt for the train. Lucca's train station offers frequent connections to towns within Cinque Terre, like Monterosso al Mare or Riomaggiore. Purchase your tickets in advance, especially during peak season.

Guided Tour: If you prefer a hassle-free experience with commentary and insights, consider a guided tour from Lucca. These tours typically include transportation, entrance fees to attractions, and sometimes even boat rides, allowing you to maximize your time in Cinque Terre.

Considering the Season: Spring and autumn boast pleasant weather, ideal for exploring the villages and hiking trails. Summers can be crowded, and boat trips might be affected by rough seas. Winters see fewer crowds but limited transportation options and potential closures due to weather.

Exploring the Cinque Terre Villages:

Cinque Terre comprises five unique villages, each with its own charm and character:

Monterosso al Mare: The largest of the five, Monterosso offers a beautiful beach, a charming historic center, and a relaxed atmosphere. Perfect for a refreshing swim or a leisurely lunch break.

Vernazza: A photographer's paradise, Vernazza boasts colorful houses cascading down a cliffside, a charming harbor, and narrow alleys perfect for wandering.

Corniglia: The only village not directly accessible by sea, Corniglia sits atop a cliff, offering stunning panoramic views. Reach it by a scenic hike or take a public shuttle from the train station.

Manarola: Famous for its colorful houses clinging to the cliffs, Manarola is a feast for the eyes. Explore its quaint harbor, charming squares, and hidden alleyways.

Riomaggiore: The southernmost village, Riomaggiore, welcomes visitors with a dramatic entrance through a tunnel. Explore its colorful main street, harbor, and don't miss the chance to capture postcard-perfect photos.

Transportation Between Villages:

Train: The train is the most efficient way to travel between villages, offering frequent connections and stunning coastal views. Purchase the Cinque Terre Card for unlimited train rides within the national park.

Ferry: During peak season (weather permitting), boat trips offer a unique perspective of the Cinque Terre coastline. Ferry services connect the villages, allowing you to admire the colorful houses from the sea.

Hiking Trails: For adventurous spirits, a network of hiking trails connects the villages. The iconic Sentiero Azzurro (Blue Trail) offers breathtaking views but requires a good level of fitness. Less challenging options are also available.

Must-See and Must-Do Experiences:

Wander the Charming Villages: Get lost in the narrow alleys, discover hidden squares, and soak up the unique atmosphere of each village.

Boat Trip: Embark on a boat trip for a different perspective of the Cinque Terre coastline. Admire the colorful houses from the sea and capture stunning photos.

Hiking Adventures: Challenge yourself with a hike on the Sentiero Azzurro or choose a shorter, more manageable trail. The panoramic views are truly rewarding.

Sample Local Delights: Indulge in fresh seafood dishes, savor local pesto pasta, and treat yourself to a refreshing gelato.

Shop for Souvenirs: Browse local shops for unique handcrafted souvenirs, like ceramics, textiles, or limoncello (a lemon liqueur).

PRACTICAL INFORMATION

- Weather and Climate
- Currency and Payment
- Language and Communication
- Safety Tips and Emergency Contacts

PRACTICAL INFORMATION

Weather and Climate

Lucca's charm extends beyond its historical walls and captivating piazzas. Its pleasant climate, with warm summers and mild winters, makes it an ideal destination year-round. Here's a comprehensive guide to help you plan your Lucca adventure based on the weather and seasonal delights:

Springtime Symphony (March-May)

Weather: Spring paints Lucca with vibrant colors as flowers bloom and temperatures rise. Expect comfortable days with highs in the low to mid 20s°C (upper 60s to low 70s°F) and occasional rain showers. Evenings can be slightly chilly, so pack a light jacket.

Things to Do: Spring is a delightful time to explore Lucca. The crowds haven't arrived yet, and the city awakens from its winter slumber. Enjoy leisurely strolls along the city walls, take a bike ride through the surrounding countryside, or participate in the many cultural events that take place during this season.

Summer Splendor (June-August)

Weather: Summer is Lucca's peak season, boasting long sunny days and warm temperatures. Averages hover in the mid to high 20s°C (upper 70s to low 80s°F), with occasional heat waves. Don't forget your sunglasses, sunscreen, and a hat! Light evening breezes cool things down, making outdoor dining a delightful experience.

Things to Do: With long sunny days, summer is perfect for exploring Lucca's piazzas, indulging in gelato breaks, and venturing outside the city walls. Day trips to nearby beaches or a boat ride on the Serchio River offer refreshing escapes from the summer heat. Lucca also comes alive with outdoor concerts, festivals, and cultural events during this season.

Autumn Tapestry (September-November)

Weather: Autumn brings a welcome change of pace. Days are still warm, with highs in the low 20s°C (upper 60s°F), but evenings become noticeably cooler. Expect occasional rain showers, so pack a light raincoat or umbrella. The changing leaves paint the Tuscan countryside in stunning shades of gold and red, making it a beautiful time for scenic walks or bike rides.

Things to Do: Autumn is a shoulder season, offering pleasant weather and fewer crowds. Enjoy exploring Lucca's museums and historical sites, indulge in leisurely shopping sprees, or take a cooking class to learn how to prepare traditional Tuscan dishes. Food festivals celebrating the autumn harvest are also a highlight of this season.

Winter Wonderland (December-February)

Weather: Winter in Lucca is mild compared to other northern European destinations. Temperatures average in the low 10s°C (mid-50s°F), with occasional dips below freezing. Rain showers are more frequent, and there might be a chance of frost or even light snowfall.

Things to Do: While the weather might not be ideal for extensive outdoor exploration, winter offers a different side of Lucca. Cozy up in charming cafes with a steaming cup of hot chocolate, explore the city's museums and churches, or attend festive Christmas markets filled with local crafts and delicious treats. Lucca's winter charm is a unique experience to savor.

Packing Tips

Spring: Pack layers for changeable weather, comfortable walking shoes, a light rain jacket, and a hat.

Summer: Pack light, breathable clothing, sunglasses, sunscreen, a hat, and a swimsuit if planning beach trips.

Autumn: Pack layers for varying temperatures, comfortable walking shoes, a light raincoat or umbrella, and a hat.

Winter: Pack warm layers, waterproof shoes, a scarf, hat, and gloves.

Currency and Payment

Money

In Italy, the official currency is the Euro (€). Euro coins are available in denominations of .01€, .02€, .05€, .10€, .20€, and .50€, as well as 1€ and 2€, while banknotes come in denominations of 5€, 10€, 20€, 50€, 100€, 200€, and 500€.

Bank machines, known as ATMs, are commonly found in most towns and cities throughout Tuscany, although they may not be as prevalent as you might expect. Therefore, it's advisable to carry some cash, especially since many smaller establishments outside the main city centers may not accept credit cards. When making small purchases, like buying a cappuccino at a bar, it's best to have smaller denominations of cash.

While traveler's checks remain a secure option, electronic banking has become increasingly popular among travelers. Bank cards and pre-paid credit cards are widely used, offering convenient access to funds.

Most hotels, restaurants, and shops in Italy accept Visa and MasterCard, with many also accepting American Express. Additionally, higher-end establishments often honor Diner's Club cards. However, it's always a good idea to carry some cash as a backup, particularly when venturing into smaller towns or rural areas.

ATM's

To ensure you get the best exchange rate when exchanging currency, it's recommended to use a bank or one of its ATMs. While the rates at currency exchange booths (known as "Cambio") may not be as favorable, they are still preferable to exchanging money at hotels or shops, which should be avoided if possible.

When traveling abroad, particularly in Italy, accessing cash from an ATM, or "Bancomat," is often the easiest and most efficient method of obtaining travel money. Before your trip, ensure that your card is enabled for international withdrawals and that you have a four-digit PIN, as most ATMs in Italy require this format.

Keep in mind that many banks charge a fee each time you use your card at an ATM belonging to another bank, and this fee may be higher for international transactions compared to domestic ones. Additionally, some banks may impose their own fee on top of this.

If you encounter a message at the ATM stating that your card isn't valid for international transactions, don't panic. Try using a different bank's ATM before becoming concerned, as this message is often a default response when the ATM is unable to read your card.

Language and Communication

Lucca, a charming Tuscan town, offers a rich tapestry of culture and history. While navigating the cobbled streets and admiring the Renaissance architecture, you'll likely encounter friendly locals. Here's a guide to understanding language and communication in Lucca to enhance your travel experience:

The Local Lingo:

Italian Reigns Supreme: Italian is the official language, and most residents speak it fluently. Though English is gaining traction in tourist areas, basic Italian phrases go a long way.

Tuscan Twang: You might hear a hint of a local dialect, Lucchhese, a variation of Tuscan Italian. It's similar to standard Italian, so you'll still be able to communicate effectively.

Essential Italian Phrases:

Greetings: "Buongiorno" (Good morning/afternoon), "Buonasera" (Good evening), "Ciao" (Hello/Goodbye - informal)

Please and Thank You: "Per favore" (Please), "Grazie" (Thank you)

Excuse Me: "Scusi" (Excuse me)

Do you speak English?: "Parla inglese?"

Numbers (1-10): Uno, Due, Tre, Quattro, Cinque, Sei, Sette, Otto, Nove, Dieci

Understanding Non-Verbal Communication:

The Power of Gesture: Italians, including Lucans, are expressive with their hands. A raised eyebrow or a dismissive hand gesture might convey more than words.

Personal Space: Italians tend to stand closer during conversations than some cultures. Don't be offended; it's considered a sign of engagement.

Communication Tips

Learn a Few Phrases: Mastering basic greetings, "grazie," and "prego" (you're welcome) shows respect and effort.

Embrace Patience: Italians prioritize conversation and building rapport. Be prepared for conversations to take a bit longer.

Speak Slowly and Clearly: If your Italian is rusty, speak slowly and enunciate clearly. Most locals will appreciate your attempt and may try to help you along.

Smile and Be Friendly: A warm smile and friendly demeanor go a long way in overcoming any language barrier.

Additional Resources:

Phrasebook: Invest in a good Italian phrasebook for handy reference on common expressions.

Translation Apps: Download a translation app to help with on-the-spot communication.

Italians are known for their hospitality. Don't be afraid to strike up a conversation, even with limited Italian.Most

Lucans will be happy to help you navigate the town and share their culture.

Safety Tips and Emergency Contacts

Staying Safe in Lucca

Lucca is renowned for its safety, but like any travel destination, it's wise to be prepared. Here's a comprehensive guide to staying safe and handling emergencies during your visit:

General Safety Precautions:

Pickpocket Awareness: Though rare, petty theft can occur in crowded areas. Keep valuables secure, avoid carrying large amounts of cash, and remain vigilant in busy places like markets and public transport. Guard Your Belongings: Never leave bags unattended, especially in cafes or restaurants. Keep a close eye on your belongings, particularly in crowded streets. Be Wary of Scams: While not prevalent, be cautious of unsolicited assistance or overly friendly strangers aiming to distract you. Trust Your Instincts: If a situation feels unsafe, remove yourself from it. Don't hesitate to seek help from trusted sources or local businesses.

Traffic Safety:

Pedestrian Priority: Lucca's city center is car-free, ideal for exploring on foot. Exercise caution when crossing streets in areas with traffic. Bicycle Safety: If cycling, wear a helmet and familiarize yourself with local traffic rules. Stick to designated bike lanes on the city walls and be cautious when crossing streets. Emergency Contacts:

European Emergency Number: Dial 112 for immediate assistance from police, ambulance, or fire services. Local Police (Polizia di Stato): For non-emergencies, contact +39 0572 24271. Carabinieri (Military Police): For non-emergencies, call +39 0572 40000. Fire Department (Vigili del Fuoco): Dial 115 in case of fire emergencies. Medical Emergencies: Head to the nearest hospital (Ospedale) or private clinic (Clinica) if medical attention is needed. The primary hospital in Lucca is "Ospedale San Luca," located at Via Nicola Matteucci, 1, reachable at +39 0572 4601.

Additional Recommendations:

Travel Insurance: Consider purchasing travel insurance to cover medical emergencies or unforeseen circumstances during your trip. Basic Italian Phrases: Learn some essential Italian phrases like "aiuto" (help), "grazie" (thank you), and "scusi" (excuse me) to assist in emergencies. By adhering to these safety guidelines and being prepared, you can enjoy a worry-free and memorable experience in Lucca.

Made in United States
Orlando, FL
15 April 2025